THE LAST GOOD MOMENT OF LILY BAKER

Russell Davis

BROADWAY PLAY PUBLISHING INC
New York
www.broadwayplaypublishing.com
info@broadwayplaypublishing.com

THE LAST GOOD MOMENT OF LILY BAKER
© Copyright 2004 by Russell Davis

Cover art by Kat O'Brien
First printing: September 2007
I S B N: 978-0-88145-356-0
Book design: Marie Donovan
Word processing: Microsoft Word
Typographic controls: Ventura Publisher
Typeface: Palatino
Printed and bound in the U S A

THE LAST GOOD MOMENT OF LILY BAKER
was produced by People's Light &Theater Company,
Malvern, PA, opening on 10 January 1990. The cast
and creative contributors were:

BOB BAKER . . . . Frank Wood
LILY BAKER . . . . Edith Meeks
SAM KASS . . . . David Ingram
MOLLY KASS . . . . Elizabeth Soukup

Director . . . . Abigail Adams
Scenic and lighting designer . . . . James F Pyne, Jr
Costume designer . . . . P Chelsea Harriman
Production stage manager . . . . Mark E Abram

THE LAST GOOD MOMENT OF LILY BAKER was
also produced by New York Stage & Film, at Vassar
College, Poughkeepsie, NY, opening on 30 June 1988.
The cast and creative contributors were:

BOB BAKER . . . . Peter Riegert
LILY BAKER . . . . Anne Twomey
SAM KASS . . . . Michael Mantell
MOLLY KASS . . . . Jayne Atkinson

Director . . . . Max Mayer
Scenic designer . . . . Thomas Kamm
Lighting designer . . . . Donald Holder
Costume designer . . . . Candice Donnelly
Production stage manager . . . . William H Lang

Earlier productions at Repertory Theater of Saint Louis, Missouri (18 January-5 February 1989); Gaslamp Quarter Theater, San Diego, California (22 October-19 December 1987); The Road Company, Johnson City, Tennessee (23-28 June 1987); Unicorn Theater, Kansas City, Missouri (14-26 April 1987)

Readings and development work at Playwrights' Center, Minneapolis; New Dramatists, N Y C; O'Neill Center's 1986 National Playwrights Conference, New London, CT; Cornell University, Ithaca, NY; George Street Playhouse, New Brunswick, NJ

CHARACTERS

BOB BAKER, *a husband in his mid-thirties*
LILY BAKER, *his wife*
SAM KASS, *his friend*
MOLLY KASS, SAM *'s wife*

These people are North Americans. They are like you and me, or maybe the way we used to be, before we thought a whole lot about what went on in this world, what caused those distant things to happen. But they are good people. They care for each other, at least BOB and LILY do. They are tentative and funny with each other. Probably slightly in awe.
And when they say, "I remember," it's not to evoke the past. It's to make a point in the present. Because they are searching for ways to greet each other again in a small room. A room that seems to have been made for a much smaller world.

Only one thing is certain. Once upon a time they used to be friends.

SETTING

A bedroom in a country inn. The bedroom is normal, except that it is somewhat sparse and out of proportion. It has pale brown walls that don't quite finish, or connect. There is a clock radio by the bed that seems larger than it should be. A sofa chair that seems slightly small. The bathroom door is much bigger than the door to the hallway. The balcony door doesn't seem to shut out the balcony. The rug in the middle of the room is very small.

Beyond the room everything is big and blue. The rest of the stage is a large, empty, blue space.

Time: The events of this play take place in June, 1980. Seven months after the takeover of the United States Embassy in Teheran by Iranian militants on November 4, 1979. There is no mention of this event in this play. There is no mention of many things in this play. But they are implicit. And in the end what's implicit, what's been there all along begins to surface. It seeps into the room and starts to look like part of the ground a person could walk on.

In the end some of these character begin to notice.

ACT ONE

Scene One

(A large bedroom in a country inn. A door to the hall, a door to the bathroom, and a door to the balcony.)

(Early afternoon. June. Enter BOB *&* LILY *from the hall.* BOB *brings their suitcases into the room.)*

(Pause)

BOB: How's it seem?

LILY: Okay.

BOB: Yeah?

LILY: It's nice.

(Pause)

BOB: Does it look the same?

LILY: Excuse me?

BOB: The same, Lily.

LILY: I don't think so.

BOB: What's different?

LILY: I don't know.

BOB: Tell me what's different.

LILY: Something, Bob, I don't know.

BOB: If you see something, you should tell me.

LILY: There's nothing I can tell you.

BOB: Okay.

LILY: Maybe it is the same.

(BOB *walks around. He looks at things.*)

LILY: Do you mind if I lie down?

BOB: Huh?

LILY: I feel very tired.

BOB: Sure. Sure, lie down.

(LILY *goes to the bed. She lies down.*)

(BOB *stops in front of a picture.*)

(*Pause*)

BOB: There he is, Lily. The Indian.

LILY: Uh huh.

BOB: The Indian on the wall. Sitting on his horse, crying to the moon. Same as last time.

LILY: Yes, Bob.

BOB: And here's the mirror. Same damn mirror. You used to brush your hair at this mirror. Still tilts, as a matter of fact.

(BOB *straightens the mirror at the dressing table. It tilts again.*)

LILY: Don't you think you should lie down?

BOB: What?

LILY: We got up early, Bob.

BOB: Nah. I want to look around.

LILY: You need to, don't you?

BOB: Lily, I'm fine without sleep. (*He stops in the middle of the room. He stands on the rug.*)

(Pause)

BOB: This is where we played Monopoly. You, me, Sam and Molly. We played Monopoly on this rug. It's the same rug.

LILY: I remember Monopoly.

BOB: And that's the chair. *(He goes to the sofa chair. He sits in it.)* This is Molly's chair. She couldn't sit in this chair. Yeah. She thought it was damp. You remember that, don't you?

LILY: No.

BOB: Molly's damp chair?

LILY No, I don't.

BOB: That's funny. I remember it clearly.

LILY: She wouldn't sit in it?

BOB: No, she wouldn't.

LILY: I don't remember.

BOB: Hm. *(He stands.)*

BOB: Molly saw spots. Didn't she also see spots? Little black things?

LILY: I think so.

BOB: Yeah, black spots. Spots in the air. They were something. She used to get faint.

LILY: I remember them.

BOB: That's good. I'm glad you remember them.

(Pause)

(BOB goes to the bathroom door. He steps into the bathroom. He steps back out.)

BOB: This is where Molly went when she saw too many spots. The bathroom. Or was it their bathroom? I think it was. I think that's what happened Molly would get up and cross the hall. Then she'd come back and her eyes would be clear.

(Pause)

BOB: How's bed?

LILY: Hm?

BOB: The bed. The bed any different?

LILY: No.

BOB: That's good. But if you notice something, let me know, okay?

LILY: Yes, Robert.

BOB: No, come on, Lily. You're better at these things than I am. You can tell in a glance if something's different.

LILY: I forgot Molly's chair.

BOB: That was psychological.

LILY: The damp chair?

BOB: Psychological, Lily. Sam made it damp. He poured bourbon.

LILY: See, I don't remember this, Bob.

BOB: I'm not talking about anything psychological. Or nasty, Lily. I'm talking about your memory for physical things.

LILY: It's not very good.

BOB: No, it is. You have an eye for physical things.

LILY: I do not.

BOB: Physical detail.

LILY: I forgot my hairbrush.

BOB: What?

LILY: I have no hairbrush.

BOB: Lily.

LILY: For the whole weekend. There's a whole weekend.

BOB: Lily, come on.

LILY: Bob, I forgot.

(Pause)

BOB: I'm not referring to things you forget to bring.
I'm referring to what concerns us. You and me,
as a couple. Cause maybe for yourself you forget.
You forget a hairbrush. But for us, as a couple,
you remember. You get us through.

LILY: Bob, if I don't have my hairbrush that will not
get us through.

BOB: No?

LILY: No. My hair will look stupid.

(LILY rolls over. She turns her back to BOB.)

BOB: Your hair will never look stupid. Your hair is
lovely.

LILY: It's stupid.

BOB: No, it's windblown. That's all. I like it windblown.
You should keep it that way.

LILY: I will.

BOB: I'm serious. I like your hair when you get out
of the car. I like it before you push it all down again.
It makes me think of college. Lots of fun and college.
Hula hoops, Lily. It's like a flag. Your hair is like a flag.
It should be out there flying. Not all folded up. Cause I
like your hair. I've always liked your hair. It makes me
think we should have gone exploring. We should have
traveled. We should have gone to the jungle, Lily. Slept

out at night, worn loincloths, something. We should
have done something before we settled.

(Pause)

BOB: I like it brushed too. There's nothing wrong with
your hair. *(He opens the balcony door. He goes out onto the
balcony. He comes back in.)* Birds.

LILY: What?

BOB: Birds out there. Nice. Good sun.

(BOB goes to MOLLY's damp chair. He sits in it.)

(LILY sits up.)

LILY: Bob, I'm sorry. You're tense, I know. I should pay
attention.

BOB: I'm not tense.

LILY: No?

BOB: No, I'm fine.

LILY: You seem tense, Bob.

BOB: I'm just anxious.

LILY: Okay.

BOB: Real anxious to be here, that's all. Glad. *(He stands.
He goes to the rug again. He stands on it.)*

(Pause)

LILY: The radio, Bob. I don't remember this radio.

BOB: Huh?

LILY: Did we have clock radios?

BOB: Back then?

LILY: It's got some kind of flag on it. A foreign flag.

BOB: *(Crossing)* What flag?

LILY: On the face. The dial.

BOB: That's Cuban.

LILY: Cuban?

BOB: Yeah, Cuban. Jesus.

LILY: How do you know that's Cuban?

BOB: Come on. You don't remember my car? My high school car. All the Cuban bumper stickers?

LILY: No.

BOB: No? What about my car radio, Lily? Remember it was stuck?

LILY: No, Bob.

BOB: I never played you the Spanish music station?

LILY: I don't think so.

BOB: You don't remember that Sam disconnected behind the knob so I couldn't change the station? So then I had to do the same thing to his parents' T V?

LILY: No, I don't.

BOB: Okay. What about the little Cuban flags I put in Sam's underwear drawer?

LILY: His underwear?

BOB: I guess this was before you and I started really going out.

LILY: Flags, Bob?

BOB: Well, he put stickers on my car.

LILY: Okay.

BOB: Come on, Lily. Sam and I weren't afraid to joke like that.

LILY: *(To herself)* I don't understand.

BOB: Lily, at the time the United States was being humiliated by Cuba. Castro, okay? Remember? Sam and I took the Bay of Pigs personally.

LILY: I guess so.

(Pause)

BOB: I guess that kind of faded. Those jokes must have faded after you and I went out.

LILY: Bob, I'm just tired.

BOB: I know.

LILY: No, I am. You should ask me later. I'll look around later and see what's changed.

BOB: That'll be good, Lily.

LILY: Because I'm sure I could see something. Some chair they moved, some picture.

BOB: You're like a canary to me.

LILY: I'll find something else.

BOB: A yellow canary. Like they had in the coal mines to warn the miners. Little birds in cages that stopped singing and fell down dead if there was a gas leak and everybody got the hell out.

(Pause. LILY lies back down.)

BOB: I don't mean it that way, Lily. That sounds ridiculous. What I mean is, for example, Sam. When Sam walks in here you'll be able to tell. Molly too. You'll know what's different about them. Like the clock radio. You'll notice something. Whereas I'll just take one look and say, hey, big deal, you guys just got back from Europe, huh, what's different?

(Pause)

BOB: I remember this rug. we played one hell of a Monopoly game on this rug.

(Pause)

*(*LILY *gets up. She goes to* MOLLY's *damp chair. She sits in it.)*

LILY: Bob, you think Sam's been to Europe, and you've never been, his kids, his wife have been to Europe, and he'll have more interesting stories? Does that make you anxious?

BOB: That I won't have stories?

LILY Well, not like Sam.

BOB: Lily, I have stories. There's lots to tell Sam.

LILY: Do you think Sam's going to be promoted?

BOB: What?

LILY: Do you think that's why they sent him to Europe?

BOB: To be promoted?

LILY: Yes.

BOB: I don't know.

(Pause)

BOB: Well. I'll let you sleep.

LILY: Where are you going?

BOB: I think outside. I want to walk around outside. I'm not really in the mood to sit around.

LILY: Bob, I don't want to sleep if you're outside.

BOB: I'll buy you a hairbrush or something.

LILY: Bob, you're upset.

BOB: No, really. Take a nap.

LILY: No, you're upset about Sam.

BOB: I'm not upset. I'm just restless.

LILY: Bob, you wanted me to be a canary.

BOB: Lily.

LILY I'm really sorry you feel it's so important to go outside.

BOB: It's not important.

LILY: Yes, it is. Every time we start to talk you go outside. I'm sick of it. I'm sick of how you go outside.

(Pause)

BOB: Wait a minute. Every time we talk, you go to sleep. How can we talk if you go to sleep?

LILY: I'm tired. I told you.

BOB: Fine. Be tired. I'm going outside.

LILY: Bob, you kept me up last night.

BOB: I did not.

LILY: Yes, you did. You were restless. You threw yourself around. You took up the whole bed.

BOB: I don't remember.

LILY: That's why I'm tired.

BOB: That's why I go outside. What's there to do in here if you're tired?

LILY: Fine. Go outside. *(She goes back to the bed. She lies down.)*

(Pause)

BOB: You see, you're much more than tired, Lily. You're disappointed. You are unexcited.

LILY I am not.

BOB: Unexcited.

LILY: I am so excited. I'm excited to be here. I think it's very nice here.

BOB: I'm not talking about here.

LILY: Then where?

BOB: I mean in general.

LILY: Well, I mean that too, Bob. I'm excited in general.
But this should help. This weekend, it should. We'll
feel better probably. We'll feel better about Sam.
Better about something.

BOB: Something has to be better?

LILY: Well, yes. There's always something, Bob.
Ask anybody.

BOB: No. You're sad.

LILY: What?

BOB: You are sad.

LILY: I am not sad.

BOB: Yes. You have become a sad person. You never
used to be so sad.

LILY: When was I sad?

BOB: For a whole year.

LILY: What year?

BOB: At least the whole last year.

LILY: Bob.

BOB: Why the hell won't you just admit, Lily? Admit it,
dammit. I mean, hell, we were happy. We started out
happy. Life was dandy. Expectant. And it pisses me off
more than anything in the world right now that you
won't even admit to me that you've changed. That
you're sad. That you, my wife, are now a goddam sad
person.

(Pause)

LILY: Why do you behave like that?

BOB: What?

LILY: Rumpelstiltskin.

BOB: Excuse me?

LILY: You heard me.

BOB: Rumpelstiltskin, Lily?

LILY: Yes, jumping up and down like that. Screaming.

BOB: Lily.

LILY: You looked very silly.

BOB: Lily, how do you manage to select something like Rumpelstiltskin?

LILY: You looked just like Rumpelstiltskin.

BOB: How the hell would you know?

LILY: There are pictures.

BOB: Pictures, huh?

LILY: Bob, he jumps up and down on the same spot.

BOB: This is ridiculous.

LILY: And he screams. Just like you.

BOB: I screamed, huh?

LILY: Yes.

BOB: Up and down too, on the same spot?

LILY: A little, yes. Right on your rug.

BOB: Well, I'm sorry.

LILY: Yes.

BOB: It must have looked silly. Did you want me to hit something?

LILY: No?

BOB: That's good. Cause that's what I was trying not to do.

LILY: Not to hit something?

BOB: Yes.

(Pause)

BOB: *(Gently)* Lily, there's nobody left in our family who wants to hear themselves compared to Rumpelstiltskin. Or to the pig that built the straw house as I heard you say to David last week. David doesn't care about that story now and Mary's not frightened by the troll who lives under the bridge. They've moved on. We've all moved on.

(Pause)

LILY: Have the kids noticed? Do they think I'm sad?

BOB: Only Mary.

LILY: She said something?

BOB: Lily, I explained that it gets harder for a mother when her kids grow up. That's all. Meanwhile David hasn't asked. David's busy.

(Pause)

(BOB *takes* MOLLY's *damp chair and brings it next to* LILY *on the bed. He sits in the chair.)*

BOB: Listen. It seems to me we shouldn't be sad. Either of us. We're together. We've done well together. And we have David. David's going to be a great big soccer star. He says so. He's going to go to Europe and play with the soccer stars. And Mary. Mary wants to be an ice skater. You've seen her. How she can glide and spin. How happy she is. Even Tumbleweed. Look at Tumbleweed. He knows how to sit. He can roll over. David showed him. Lily, we're doing well. There're these little individuals in our house and they're happy.

LILY: Bob, I have no right to be sad. I never, ever planned on being sad.

BOB: Then what's making you?

LILY: I don't know.

BOB: Be specific.

LILY: No, Bob, not everybody's like you.

BOB: Okay.

LILY: Not everybody can be specific.

(Pause)

(LILY sits on the edge of the bed. She regards the clock radio. She gets up.)

LILY: I'm going to look around.

BOB: Good.

(LILY walks around the room.)

(BOB takes a piece of paper out of his pocket. He looks at it.)

BOB: This is a note yesterday from Arthur Bettelheim.

LILY: Arthur Bettelheim?

BOB: The Chairman of Engelbetter, Lily.

LILY: Yes, of course.

BOB: It says, Thank you, you're doing a good job.

LILY: That's nice.

BOB: It's a form note, Lily.

LILY: Yes?

BOB: I don't know what I did to get this form note.

LILY: Maybe it's a good sign.

BOB: Hm.

(LILY comes to a stop in front of a wall.)

LILY: Bob. I've noticed something else. The calendar.

BOB: What about the calendar?

LILY: It's different.

BOB: Lily, they can change the calendar.

LILY: It says 1965.

BOB: It does?

LILY: That's right. It has a wooden covered bridge and it says 1965.

(BOB *comes and looks at the calendar. Pause)*

BOB: I think it's the same calendar. *(He goes to the phone. He dials.)* See what happens when you get up, Lily, and look around? See, when you're not so tired? *(Into phone)* Hello, this is Bob Baker. My wife and I are up here in our room, which is very nice, but we just noticed the calendar...We don't think you've changed the calendar. Do you guys down there agree it's 1980? We're in 1980? ...Excuse me? ...Oh, really? *(He turns and faces the bookcase. He picks up a magazine. Into phone)* Yes, you're right. *(To LILY) Time* magazine, Lily. They do this on purpose. *(Into phone)* Yes, I can see. June 25, 1965... Well, thank you... Yes, we appreciate the effort. The memory, yes. Thank you. We'll see you soon. *(He hangs up.)* No wonder these places are so expensive.

LILY: They have us listed from before?

(BOB *goes through the bookcase. He finds something.)*

BOB: Lily. Lily, look. This is you and me.

LILY: Yes?

BOB: Look. We're getting married. Sam and Molly too.

LILY: Oh, yes.

BOB: Look, Lily. Football. Baseball programs. Look, that's you. You and all your pompoms. And there's Sam. Here's Sam and I painting my parents' house.

LILY: Yes, I see.

BOB: We're standing on ladders. See, with buckets?

LILY: *(Taking another photograph)* What's this?

BOB: What's what?

LILY: Sam's on the ground.

BOB: Oh, yeah. He fell.

LILY: Why's he smiling on the ground?

BOB: He fell off the ladder, remember? Knocked himself out.

LILY: But he's smiling.

BOB: He wanted a picture before he got up.

LILY: I thought he was unconscious.

BOB: He's fine. Look at him. Everything's fine.

LILY: *(To herself)* I don't understand this photograph.

BOB: I don't understand any of these photographs. I mean, how the hell does this hotel have this stuff? Where did they find this, huh?

(Pause)

(They look at the clock radio. They look at the programs and photographs.)

LILY: Sam must have arranged it. Sam. He must have sent them things.

BOB: I don't know, Lily.

LILY: I don't like this.

BOB: Yeah, I guess Sam. That's Sam. Sam probably guessed we could argue. Coming back to a place like this could make two people argue. So Sam just sent this fun stuff, this happy memory stuff, Lily, to cheer us up. Keep us happy.

LILY: I think Laurie came here.

BOB: Laurie didn't come here.

LILY: Your secretary, Bob. She used to work for Sam.

BOB: So?

LILY: So Sam called her. Told her where to find these things.

(Pause)

BOB: Well, that's great, if that happened. I think that's great. See, leaving Laurie to me in the first place, that was great.

LILY: Bob, you said to me last week you didn't like taking anything from Sam. Especially a pre-trained secretary.

BOB: I said that? I said pre-trained?

LILY: You did.

BOB: I must have been in a bad mood if I said that. I can't imagine saying that.

LILY: Well, you did. Pre-trained.

BOB: I get in these moods.

LILY: You're in one now.

BOB: A bad mood?

LILY: Very bad, yes. You're trying to be positive.

BOB: I'm not positive.

LILY: Yes, because Sam is coming back and that's supposed to be great.

BOB: It is great.

LILY: I think you're developing a headache.

BOB: My head is fine.

LILY: Bob, really, there is one thing that bothers me about you and that is Sam.

BOB: I don't have a headache.

LILY: Your history with Sam. You can't say anything negative about Sam, or imply anything, that you won't deny later.

BOB: I don't deny anything.

LILY: Yes, you do.

BOB: I just don't remember.

LILY: What's the big difference?

BOB: Listen, Lily, if I say something in a bad mood, like for instance about Sam, it means just that: I was in a bad mood. Especially if I can't remember later. And the same applies to you. It applies to everybody. I say things and I get into bad moods. Big deal. Moods pass. *(He exits into the bathroom.)*

(Pause. He comes back out.)

LILY: Okay. I'm in a bad mood.

BOB: I know.

LILY: I may not remember this.

BOB: Okay.

LILY: I don't trust Sam. I have never trusted Sam. I don't think you understand a thing about Sam.

BOB: Of course I understand.

LILY: No, you guys were supposed to be equal.

BOB: What?

LILY: Equal forever.

BOB: There was nothing equal.

LILY: Equal buddies, yes.

BOB: No, I was always better, I mean basically better at what counted, what went on, like school, when we grew up. Whereas Sam had plans.

LILY: He changed them, Bob.

BOB: Sam had imagination.

LILY: He changed the plan, Bob, when he saw you with me.

BOB: Lily.

LILY: No, that's true, Sam went to the big world. To a university. He didn't stay around and be equal, equal buddies, and go to a state college. Why don't you just admit that? And I think Sam decided he could come back, I think he decided we could all get married together, so he could show off Molly to you. So he could have Molly and me, side by side in bridal gowns, and he could show off Molly to you.

(Pause)

BOB: Lily, this is pretty big for a mood.

LILY: It's what I think.

BOB: You're not thinking. You're being sensitive.

LILY: No, Bob. Molly's very sophisticated.

BOB: This is silly.

LILY: Pretty too.

BOB: You're not pretty?

LILY: Not sophisticated pretty.

BOB: She sees spots, for heaven's sake.

LILY: But they're like a handkerchief. She drops them like a handkerchief. She makes you want to swat the air for her. Molly is a big asset to Sam.

BOB: What asset?

LILY: She's outgoing. Molly is very outgoing.

BOB: No, you're outgoing yourself, Lily. You were the most outgoing, wonderful, charming woman in the whole of our town.

LILY: That's not true.

BOB: It is. You were.

LILY: If it is, I stopped.

BOB: You didn't stop.

LILY: I did. I stopped being outgoing. I can no longer ever again be so outgoing.

(Pause)

BOB: Big deal. I used to be more outgoing too. I used to be one hell of a guy. Some kind of local hero. I guess we affected each other. That's all. We can't keep up. We can't keep up with all these outgoing people. These Mollys from the big world.

(Pause)

LILY: Bob, I used to ask questions and pay attention, remember? I used to do that all the time. It used to feel so good I was your wife, and when I asked your friends questions, it felt good, and when I put them at ease, it made me feel so good....

(Pause)

BOB: Lily, I used to know what you were thinking. I could tell pretty much what was on your mind. There was a feeling we were united. The same mind. But you're hanging back now. I don't know what you're thinking.

(Pause)

LILY: I'm ashamed. That's all.

BOB: Ashamed?

LILY: I feel ashamed.

BOB: What did you do to make you ashamed?

LILY: Nothing.

BOB: Nothing? What's nothing? No other men, nothing like that?

LILY: I've done nothing.

BOB: Then what's the shame?

LILY: I just feel it.

BOB: Damn, Lily. Don't you ever, can't you ever figure anything out?

LILY: Yes.

BOB: Then figure it out. Tell me what the hell's going on. You've got to get specific, Lily. Life is specific. It's not just shame. Something triggers shame. Lily, do you understand? Do you hear? It's crazy if you don't get specific and tell me what the shame is.

(Pause)

LILY: I've been seeing buffalo, Bob.

BOB: Huh?

LILY: Buffalo.

BOB: Buffalo, honey?

LILY: I see them.

BOB: What do you mean, you see them?

LILY: I see buffalo when I shouldn't see buffalo.

BOB: Is there a time when you shouldn't see them?

LILY: Yes. When they don't exist.

BOB: Oh.

LILY: I see them when they're not there.

BOB: Okay.

LILY: It makes me ashamed.

BOB: Lily, buffalo exist.

LILY: Not these ones.

BOB: No, they have buffalo. Buffalo farms even out east.

LILY: These buffalo cross the roads.

BOB: What?

LILY: That's what they do.

BOB: They got loose?

LILY: No, they don't exist. And they cross the roads. They even stand sometimes in the middle of the road. Grazing.

BOB: Grazing, huh?

LILY: Bob, I've been seeing buffalo when I drive. When I take the kids swimming, or David to soccer, after I drop them off, on the way back I see buffalo. Or on the way to the store. It makes it very difficult to drive.

(Pause)

BOB: You see buffalo?

LILY: That's what I see.

BOB: That's a little absurd, isn't it?

LILY: I don't know why I see buffalo.

BOB: Honey, I don't either.

LILY: But I see them. They roam.

BOB: They're not spots?

LILY: These are buffalo, Bob. They're out there roaming. They pay no attention to our roads, or the fences, anything. They walk right through them. Buildings, people, fences. Right through them.

BOB: Does anybody say anything?

LILY: No, nobody notices.

BOB: Uh huh.

LILY: Just me.

BOB: How about now?

LILY: I don't see them now.

BOB: That's good.

LILY: I don't ever see them when you're around.

BOB: No?

LILY: You seem to disperse them.

BOB: Uh huh.

LILY: They don't come into our house either. But it's getting to the point where I don't want to look out the windows. Bob, I don't know how much longer the house is going to be safe for me. Or the children. I don't think they're going to stay away from the children. I think they're going to start roaming right through our whole house even, and right through you, Bob. And then nothing will be safe. I won't be safe.

(Pause)

BOB: Honey, I'm starting to feel very strange.

LILY: I can't seem to stay on my side of the road anymore.

BOB: What?

LILY: Yes. Or I stop the car.

BOB: You stop for what, for buffalo? What about the other cars?

LILY: They drive right through them.

BOB: Oh, man.

LILY: It's okay. They stop for me.

BOB: What's okay?

LILY: It is. I pretend I'm stalled. The car's stalled.
Meanwhile the buffalo move pretty fast. I don't have
to stop for long. Not long at all. Most of the time,
almost all the time, I just slow down. Or weave.
I just weave to avoid them.

BOB: Weave, Lily?

LILY: Bob.

BOB: What about driving right through them, Lily?
Did it ever occur to you that maybe you should just
drive right through and then maybe they wouldn't
bother you anymore? They'd go away?

LILY: No, they wouldn't, Bob.

BOB: No, they would. I tell you you're always too soft
with things. Too scared to hurt something. The kids.
The dog. But in this case you're not going to hurt a
damn thing.

LILY: I've done that.

BOB: You're going to drive through a hallucination.

LILY: I did that all the time at first.

BOB: You drove through?

LILY: I hear a scream.

BOB: What scream?

LILY: I don't know what scream, Bob. I just hear a
scream. And it doesn't stop till I stop. So it's better
if I stop ahead of the scream, I can stop the car better,
because the scream is very distracting.

(Pause)

LILY: I need help, Bob.

BOB: Come on.

LILY: Maybe a hospital.

BOB: No, come on, everything's okay. The car's okay.

LILY: It's been a year.

BOB: This has?

LILY: Over a year.

BOB: And you didn't tell me?

LILY: I wanted them to leave.

BOB: But, honey.

LILY: I wanted to hold up my end.

BOB: What end?

LILY: My end, Bob.

BOB: *(Angry)* If you get yourself killed on the road, Lily, that's not holding up your end.

(Pause)

(They embrace.)

LILY: I should have told you.

BOB: Why don't you lie down for now? We should rest. Come on, let's get us some rest.

(BOB helps LILY lie down on the bed. He sits in the chair next to her.)

LILY: You don't want to go outside?

BOB: No, Lily.

LILY: That's nice.

BOB: You feel better?

LILY: I can be outgoing again, Bob.

BOB: Sure.

LILY: Just give me some time.

BOB: That's right, Lily. You take your time.

(BOB *strokes* LILY's *hair.*)

BOB: I can keep the buffalo away, honey. You watch me. You let me know if you hear one of those screams.

LILY: Okay.

BOB: I can hold them off.

LILY: Thank you.

BOB: I'm still young enough for that.

LILY: I know.

BOB: Yeah, just you wait. Sam's going to walk in, Lily, and Molly, and they're not going to notice one bit of difference. We're going to look the same. Exactly the same to them. Like nothing's different.

(*There is a loud click.*)

(BOB & LILY *look at the clock radio next to them.*)

(*The sound of someone singing in Spanish on the radio.*)

Scene Two

(*The next morning*)

(BOB *is alone in the room. He is awake in bed.*)

(*There is a knock on the door.* BOB *gets out of bed. He crosses to the door and opens it.* SAM *walks in.*)

BOB: Sam.

SAM: Hi, Bob.

BOB: Sam, what are you doing?

SAM: Where's Lily?

BOB: Lily's out.

SAM: Oh, yeah?

BOB: Out walking, yeah.

SAM: Well, Molly's sleeping. You want coffee?

BOB: Coffee?

SAM: Yeah, come on, get out of those pajamas.
Get dressed.

BOB: No, I got to wait for Lily.

SAM: She can see us downstairs.

BOB: I don't think so, Sam. Thanks.

SAM: Something wrong with Lily?

BOB: Nothing wrong, no. She likes walking.
Mornings make her walk.

SAM: Good.

BOB: She's fine.

SAM: Can I keep you company then? Can I sit?

BOB: Excuse me?

SAM: Yeah, we can wait together for Lily. My wife's
sleeping, yours is out walking, I think now is a good
time for company. *(He sits.)*

(Pause)

*(BOB closes the door. He goes to the balcony. He closes the
balcony door.)*

SAM: Some night, huh?

BOB: Hm?

SAM: Last night.

BOB: *(Going back to bed)* Yeah.

SAM: I thought you were great last night. We had a great time last night.

BOB: Thanks.

SAM: Molly and I, both of us. Even Molly agreed.

BOB: Well, Lily too.

SAM: That's a damn fine restaurant they have downstairs.

BOB: Yep.

SAM: Damn fine. I feel pretty goddam good we selected to come back here. I think it adds to the pleasure of seeing each other again.

BOB: I think so too.

SAM: It's a pity Lily got so tired, that's all. Cause I could have kept on going.

BOB: Sure.

SAM: Followed you guys right up to this room and kept on going. Molly too. She told me. She said what the hell are we going to bed now for?

BOB: It's the country.

SAM: That's what I told her, Bob. The country.

BOB: Good.

SAM: Anyway, here we are. The country. Our memories. Our marriages. Everything. Lots of things out there. Lots to be glad about.

(BOB *gets out of bed. He goes to the balcony door. He opens it.*)

(*Pause*)

SAM: I got a phone call this morning from Beaver, for christsakes.

BOB: Beaver?

SAM: Yeah, Beaver. He called the room just now. He's concerned, Bob, about keeping me in Europe.

BOB: *(Going back to bed)* Who's Beaver?

LILY: You don't know Beaver?

BOB: Never heard of him.

SAM: Come on, Bob, you know Beaver Bettelheim.

BOB: Beaver Bettelheim?

SAM: Sure, Arthur Bettelheim. We call him Beaver.

BOB: You call the head of our company Beaver?

SAM: It's a nickname.

BOB: Beaver?

SAM: Come on, Bob, he chews pencils, who knows? It's what we call him.

BOB: I wouldn't know. I just get notes.

SAM: Notes?

BOB: Little form notes, yeah, saying, good job.

SAM: That's nice.

BOB: They don't sign them "Beaver."

SAM: Well, I have to call him something.

BOB: Beaver, huh?

SAM: That's right.

BOB: So Beaver calls you on weekends like this?

SAM: Well, if he wakes up thinking about something. Sure. My safety, for one thing. We have to discuss my safety.

BOB: What safety?

SAM: Bob, they have madmen in Europe. Groups of madmen.

BOB: I know.

SAM: Much more than here. We just have single people here.

BOB: Uh huh.

SAM: Individuals. Somebody who'll haul off and do a multiple murder. Some ordinary guy. But over there, Bob, they have groups. Whole groups who can dismember you. Put you in a garbage bag. Call the Embassy, for christsakes. You're pretty aware of these groups in Europe. As a matter of fact, Beaver suggested this morning I hire some security.

BOB: Security, huh?

SAM: Yeah, for the office. But also when I travel, like to the Middle East or something. There's going to be a guy traveling with me. A plainclothes man.

BOB: Uh huh.

SAM: I'm telling you, Bob, it's a problem out there. Big problem. We had no idea when we were young.

(BOB *gets out of bed. He goes to the balcony door. He closes it.*)

(*Pause*)

SAM: What's the matter with you and the door?

BOB: I don't know. It got cold.

SAM: You just opened the damn thing.

BOB: I thought it was hot.

SAM: Bob, you seem disheveled.

BOB: I'm not disheveled.

SAM: I'm concerned.

BOB: I'm still in bed.

SAM: Lily got you up too early?

BOB: Sam, I'm fine. Keep talking. (*He picks up a shirt.
He puts it on.*)

SAM: You worried about the weekend, or something?

BOB: What about it?

SAM: Well, it's long. I mean, we're kind of on top of
each other for a couple of days.

BOB: I'm not worried, no.

SAM: Well, there's time. You worried about filling the
time?

BOB: No.

SAM: How about the girls? All this time with the girls.
That bother you?

BOB: No, as a matter of fact, I want more time.

SAM: Yeah?

BOB: With Lily, sure. Lily and I need more time.
We decided.

SAM: That's good.

BOB: More weekends together.

SAM: Uh huh.

(*Pause*)

(BOB *opens the balcony door.*)

BOB: Birds.

SAM: Huh?

BOB: There's birds out there. I didn't want to miss the
birds.

SAM: That's nice.

BOB: Maybe I'm just bad in the morning, Sam. I don't
talk well in the morning. That's one reason Lily goes
for walks. Morning walks.

SAM: Uh huh.

BOB: How about you?

SAM: I'm fine in the morning.

BOB: Yeah?

SAM: Just fine.

BOB: I found it easier last night, Sam. We talked well last night.

SAM: I know.

BOB: With Molly and Lily around. That was easier.

SAM: It was fun, yeah.

BOB: And it's a good restaurant.

SAM: Sure.

BOB: A good restaurant. We should do that again.

SAM: Let's do it tonight, Bob.

BOB: Wasn't I always kind of silent anyway in the morning?

SAM: No. You used to be articulate.

BOB: In the morning?

SAM: Very articulate, Bob.

BOB: Hm.

SAM: Perky. I remember.

BOB: Perky, gee. Maybe we should have done this at home. Met at home. Instead of trying to be so goddam special. I could have walked you around town and showed you how everything's all changed. Cause there's lots. Lots of change. Take Levy's, for example, that's gone. Jeez, it's nowhere. It's a great big road now. A highway. We could stand in the middle of this highway and look at the mall, the big changes. The big everything. But in here, this room, Sam, it shouldn't feel so different. The only thing different, the only change, should be I could take one look at you now and say, hey, big deal, you guys just got back from Europe, huh, what's different? *(He pushes the balcony door shut with his foot. He goes back to the bed. He takes off his pajama bottoms. He puts on trousers.)* I woke up wrong, Sam. I must have woken up wrong.

SAM: Well, we celebrated. We drank.

BOB: That's right. We drank too much.

SAM: You're hung over.

BOB: Yeah, I didn't realize I was hung over. I thought I went to bed early.

SAM: Maybe I'm hung over too.

BOB: You think so?

SAM: Yeah, I feel edgy.

BOB: Well, we're not so young anymore. *(He exits into the bathroom.)*

(Pause)

(SAM crosses. He leans against the wall outside the bathroom.)

SAM: Maybe, Bob, there's some kind of pressure going on.

BOB: *(From off)* What pressure?

SAM: Screwed up pressure, that's all. For example, maybe one of us has changed. That kind of pressure.

BOB: *(Emerging from the bathroom)* Yeah.

SAM: Whereas there shouldn't be any pressure. Any need to entertain. Cause we have a history together. A track record. We can sit back and let our history take over. The things we used to do. That can take over and take care of us.

BOB: You're right. (*He looks around the room. He goes and sits down in* MOLLY's *chair.*)

(*Pause*)

BOB: Molly's chair. Remember you poured bourbon in this chair?

SAM: That's the chair?

BOB: I believe so.

SAM: I remember.

BOB: A lot of bourbon, Sam.

SAM: Well, she deserved it.

BOB: I can't remember why.

SAM: She said it was damp.

BOB: No, I think there was something before.

SAM: I can't remember.

BOB: She used to say a lot of stuff.

SAM: She still does. Little remarks.

BOB: Yeah, you could get enthusiastic about something.

SAM: That's right. And she'd poke a hole in it.

BOB: She was sophisticated.

SAM: Un-American.

BOB: Which is fine.

SAM: Molly's fine now.

BOB: I just wasn't sure why you married her.

SAM: She was the big world, Bob.

BOB: I guess so.

SAM: A challenge. Our little town humor didn't work on her.

BOB: I think it only worked on us, Sam. You can't blame Molly.

SAM: Well.

BOB: We must have been stupid that night.

SAM: Sure, two guys getting married. That's stupid.

BOB: No, we were probably pretty goofy in general.

SAM: We were enthusiastic.

BOB: A lot of that stuff, I look back, it's goofy.

SAM: Simple hearted.

BOB: Goofy.

SAM: Goofy, fine. That's what happens when you're young. You get together on goofy stuff.

BOB: I guess.

SAM: But if there's something underneath it'll last. It'll mature. We had something underneath. I mean, it's easy as all hell to look back and notice that some of the things that gave us goosebumps back then are actually a little ridiculous now.

BOB: Sure, like John Foster Dulles. Eisenhower.

SAM: Well, no, I like Dulles.

BOB: The Marines landing in the Dominican Republic.

SAM: I don't think that was so bad either.

BOB: Well, what do you think?

SAM: I just remember a lot of goosebumps, Bob. I remember feeling pride. That there was a right and clear way. That's all. That's what seems so goofy now.

BOB: Yeah.

SAM: Seems more complex. A hell of a lot more complex.

BOB: It was pretty complex back then. I mean, Molly was complex.

SAM: You're right.

BOB: The chair. This chair was complex.

SAM: Entirely too complex.

BOB: Well, you cleared that one up fast.

SAM: I did. I remember.

BOB: As a matter of fact, that was the first time I realized you could take charge. I didn't know you could do that. Take charge like that.

SAM: You mean with Molly?

BOB: Well, no, in general.

SAM: In general, really? You mean I used to kind of tag along?

BOB: Well, I don't know, Sam.

SAM: Like the time we painted your parents' house?

BOB: You tagged along?

SAM: Yeah, the time I fell.

BOB: Yeah, I'm sorry.

SAM: It's okay. It's fine. We grew up together, that's what I remember.

BOB: Uh huh. Besides, yeah, you're different now.

SAM: I think so.

BOB: Seem very different.

SAM: Yeah. Yeah, it's different now.

(Pause)

(They stand in the middle of the room. They look down at the rug.)

BOB: Where did we get that English Monopoly board?

SAM: Molly. Her parents brought it back from England.

BOB: Oh, yeah?

SAM: I took it.

BOB: Do you think about that game?

SAM: I do. I think how my best friend and I got married and stayed up playing Monopoly.

BOB: Yeah, on three boards.

SAM: That's right. We could borrow too.

BOB: Spanish, English and American.

SAM: We could borrow as much as we could build.

BOB: Except for interest.

SAM: Interest, yeah. Interest at "GO".

BOB: Three "GO"s.

SAM: Right, three "GO"s. Lots of interest. Three governments too, weren't there?

BOB: Wasn't "GO" the airport?

SAM: Tariffs. Remember tariffs? And remember Molly didn't like all the different regulations? The customs?

BOB: She wanted regular rules.

SAM: So we took her to court.

BOB: I thought you took me to court.

SAM: That was later. We took Molly. She wouldn't pay taxes.

BOB:But you took me, right?

SAM: Sure, cause you got ahead.

BOB: I know. You declared me mentally incompetent to handle my property.

SAM: Yeah, well, it's a good story.

BOB: No, I know.

SAM: It helps people relax.

BOB: What people?

SAM: People visiting the office in Milan. Business clients, associates.

BOB: You tell it to people?

SAM: Sure, they relax when I tell that story. Cause it's personal. Talking about your honeymoon like that. That's personal.

BOB: Uh huh.

SAM: It's important, Bob, to keep a personal touch to all your business transactions.

BOB: Sure.

SAM: Very important.

(Pause)

BOB: How are Molly's spots, by the way?

SAM: Spots, Bob?

BOB: Didn't she used to see spots?

SAM: Spots, right. They're gone.

BOB: What?

SAM: All gone. Europe's too exciting for spots.

BOB: That's great. That must be great.

SAM: She's much better now.

BOB: Yeah, she seemed better. Didn't go to the bathroom once.

SAM: Excuse me?

BOB: The bathroom. Remember she used to go to the bathroom? Molly seemed very comfortable last night.

SAM: Yeah, I hated those spots.

BOB: You did not.

SAM: Sure, I did. They used to strike her in the middle of an argument. Come down from nowhere, they'd come down out of the air.

BOB: No, I always thought Molly was kind of charming.

SAM: She encouraged the damn things.

BOB: Come on, they were ladylike.

SAM: Bob, listen, it's easy to be attracted to a beautiful woman who sees spots. It's different to live with them.

BOB: Yeah.

SAM: I just had to knock the spots out of her. That's all. Now we're fine. Instead of spots, Molly sees opera. La Scala. Which I think looks good on her. Good on me too. Because, quite frankly, Molly's pretty good for a wife.

BOB: That's nice.

SAM: As a matter of fact, I was telling somebody the other day what I feel about Molly. An associate, an Italian buddy of mine, I told him I take my wife out. Because she charms people. You should see how she can charm. How she dangles herself. Dangles her ankles. Her conversation. She leaves off words so that men can rush up and finish her sentences for her. They like to do that in Europe. They like to finish a pretty lady's thoughts for her. A pretty lady adds a mystery to things. A sense of possibility. My wife's good at that. I appreciate that. Cause what it does, Bob, is it reflects on me. I have this wife. Molly. And it does something to me. Something to my appeal. People want to work with me.

BOB: Uh huh.

SAM: But don't get me wrong, Bob. I was just as glad last night that Lily got tired. Cause Molly was about to get snippy. I could see it in her eyes. And sometimes I think the spots are gone, but there are other things now. For example, Molly hears snickers these days.

BOB: Snickers?

SAM: Yeah, snickering. Molly likes to tell me that people snicker behind my back. They titter. For example, yesterday Molly explained to me that the people downstairs were snickering.

BOB: What people?

SAM: At the desk.

BOB: The people at the desk snickered at you?

SAM: According to Molly.

BOB: Do you think they did?

SAM: No, I don't think they did. I just think she wants them to.

BOB: Uh huh.

SAM: She's difficult, Bob. She can be charming. Last night she was charming. But today she could be like a Doberman.

BOB: A Doberman?

SAM: A Doberman pinscher, yeah. A dog that doesn't snooze. Won't nap. Instead it watches you, Bob. It paces. Like it's in captivity.

(Pause)

(SAM opens the balcony door. He closes it.)

SAM: So. How's Laurie? Your secretary, Bob.

BOB: Laurie's fine.

SAM: She working out well for you? You didn't mind, did you?

BOB: No, I didn't mind.

SAM: She's a good gal. Hell, I couldn't do this stuff from Italy. This high school stuff.

BOB: No, as far as I'm concerned, Laurie should call in sick more often.

SAM: What for?

BOB: She seems a little bored sometimes. That's all.

SAM: Laurie?

BOB: Yeah, I think she gets bored.

SAM: Come on, Bob. How can Laurie be bored?

BOB: Well, reluctant.

SAM: What kind of stuff do you use her for?

BOB: Secretarial.

SAM: Secretary stuff? Bob, Laurie has imagination. A mind.

BOB: No, I know.

SAM: No, she can be your partner. Your aide-de-camp.

BOB: Aide-de-what?

SAM: De camp. Your spy.

BOB: My spy?

SAM: Secretary is just a cover. Laurie can function as your spy.

BOB: I don't think of her as a spy.

SAM: Well, start thinking that way. No wonder she's bored.

BOB: Since when was my secretary a spy?

SAM: Bob. Bob, I used to have clients come in, competitors, whatever. And if it was important to me, Laurie would go out, have dinner with someone. She'd bring back the kind of information, even just an inside impression, I would never get myself. She can pretend to someone she's dissatisfied with me, with her job, her job's on the line, whatever. Or to somebody else she's happy. Because, Bob, men are stupid when it comes to a pretty girl.

BOB: I guess so.

SAM: Laurie was my partner. She knew the potential of what she could do.

BOB: Make men stupid?

SAM: Yeah, create scenes. Distractions. Appeal to the enemy male ego.

BOB: You paid extra for this?

SAM: You bet I did. Laurie is a legitimate company expense. Furthermore, part of going up in this company is having access to funds you don't quite have to explain.

BOB: I didn't know that.

SAM: Well, now you do.

BOB: Thanks.

SAM: But don't be a jerk about it. Do it well. Do it subtly and graciously and eventually someone like Bettelheim will notice. I gave you Laurie so you could start picking up the idea.

BOB: I guess I didn't understand.

SAM: She tried to explain it, didn't she?

BOB: Yeah. Yeah, I guess she probably did.

SAM: And what did you say?

BOB: I said I didn't like it. I thought it was dishonest.

SAM: Oh.

(Pause)

SAM: Well, that's a whole other issue.

BOB: Yeah.

SAM: Honesty.

BOB: Sure.

SAM: I don't think honesty has a thing to do with what we do.

BOB: No?

SAM: No, we work for a corporation. We work for a team. The only thing dishonest is if we screw up the team. Laurie knows how to be your team and I'm sorry you didn't understand that.

BOB: Maybe you should have explained it to me.

SAM: Maybe so.

BOB: Given me the owner's manual. The Laurie manual.

(Pause)

(SAM opens the balcony door.)

SAM: I guess I was just working it out, Bob. As I went along. And you were fine. Just fine. I thought, okay, that's how Bob does fine. People respect, they know, Bob's straightforward. He means what he says and that's rare. And quite frankly, Bob, I couldn't tell you before I went away to Milan for three years. It might have alienated you. So I said to myself, everything's fine. Bob'll be fine. I'll give him Laurie. Laurie'll slowly get him going again.

(Pause)

BOB: Has Laurie ever said anything?

SAM: About what?

BOB: About me. Do you ask her about me?

SAM: No, I ask you about you.

BOB: Come on. Every time you call, you seem to talk to her.

SAM: Bob, that's old times. We talk.

BOB: Does she say she's bored?

SAM: No. No, Laurie never mentions that.

BOB: Come on, Sam, damn, you got her the job. You're responsible if she's bored.

SAM: Bob.

BOB: So she must mention something. That's her forte.

SAM: What's her forte?

BOB: Inside information.

SAM: Now, Bob, hold it, ho. Laurie never said she was bored. She never said that.

BOB: Sure, cause you guys have your own language.

SAM: What language?

BOB: Code language. There's a code for bored.

SAM: Bob, I guessed, okay?

BOB: Probably just "Bob". Plain "Bob" means bored.

SAM: What the hell's the problem here? You don't even like her as a secretary.

BOB: It's the principle of the thing.

SAM: What principle?

BOB: She's working for you. She's pre-trained.

SAM: No, Bob.

BOB: She's not working for me. She's bored with me.

SAM: Yeah, so?

BOB: So where's this lady's real spirit? It's tough, Sam, to find out that your secretary actually has a past history as a spy. I mean, I feel like some kind of cuckold. Not a cuckold, a real cuckold, but some kind of mental connection to a cuckold. Some kind of corporate derivative of a cuckold. Because basically I feel deceived. Like my secretary has gone elsewhere for excitement. That that bored Lois Lane look-a-like in my office is a mere shell of herself. My office has been attended to by a mere shell ever since the day her Superman flew to Italy.

(Pause)

(SAM closes the balcony door.)

SAM: I think we'd feel better if we had some coffee.

BOB: Yeah?

SAM: Downstairs there's coffee.

BOB: I don't want to go downstairs.

SAM: You don't want to put on some shoes?

BOB: I'm fine without shoes.

SAM: Fine. How much longer do we hang around for Lily?

BOB: You don't have to wait.

SAM: I'm your buddy. I'll wait.

BOB: Fine.

(Pause)

SAM: Bob, one of the things I've been wondering about is maybe Laurie should go to Italy with me.

BOB: Oh, yeah?

SAM: I think I need Laurie with me.

BOB: That's fine. I make her bored.

SAM: No. You just didn't realize.

BOB: Uh huh.

SAM: Maybe I should mention it to Beaver.

BOB: Beaver?

SAM: Yeah, Bettelheim.

BOB: Mention what to Beaver?

SAM: That maybe Laurie should go to Italy.

BOB: Mention, huh?

SAM: Sure.

BOB: In passing or something? Over tea? Over a morning breakfast call? Gee, Sam.

SAM: Bob.

BOB: What is this Beaver Bettelheim bullshit?

SAM: What bullshit?

BOB: Sam, it used to be Bettelheim was a distant C E O. Now all of a sudden he's Beaver to you. Some kind of table tennis buddy.

SAM: Bob.

BOB: No, Sam, if you're on some kind of terms with this man, just tell me. Tell me. Don't however drop his name like it's some kind of golden tangerine. Don't dangle Beaver at me from your mouth. And about the security, Sam. Why don't you tell me? Tell me it's a big deal. Don't try to mention it casually. Don't try to make

me think you're used to it. Like you had a plainclothes
man entourage ever since the day you were born.
Like you were some kind of Kennedy. Because I know
better. We used to shop together at Levy's. But as far
as you're concerned, that's buried. That's past. You and
Molly shop in Milano, Italy now. And that's great. Must
feel great to come back here and greet your old buddy.
Great to bury him. Great to get him the hell out of your
mind.

SAM: I came to bury?

BOB: You bet.

SAM: Bury what, Bob?

BOB: Screw you, Sam. This weekend is homage. Mere
homage to what we used to be.

(Pause)

SAM: I don't think a damn thing's buried. For example,
what's this? *(He goes to the clock radio. He turns it on.)*

(The sound of someone singing in Spanish)

SAM: Did you take the time to do this? Or the calendar?
All these programs, this high school stuff, did you do
any of this? This picture. This picture of me on the
ground smiling? No, you didn't. Cause you call it
buried. The whole thing buried. And what about this,
you horse's ass? *(He starts to unbuckle his pants.)*

BOB: What are you doing, Sam?

SAM: I'm showing you my underwear.

BOB: I don't want to see your underwear, Sam.

SAM: You're seeing it anyway.

BOB: What for?

SAM: Cause I wore them for you. *(Showing his
underwear)* What do you see?

BOB: Your underwear.

SAM: What color underwear?

BOB: Looks Cuban.

SAM: You bet, Cuban. This has got the Cuban flag all over it. I had these underwear printed up in Milan just for you.

BOB: Thanks.

SAM: I mean, goddammit, there was a time when you were like Zorba the Greek to me.

BOB: What?

SAM: Zorba. You were the Zorba in our town.

BOB: I don't remember this.

SAM: No, you wouldn't. Cause it's buried to you, you stupid ass.

(SAM *yanks the clock radio out of the wall. Music stops.* SAM *heads toward the balcony door with the radio.)*

(The hallway door opens. Enter LILY.*)*

(Pause)

LILY: Sam?

BOB: Sam's showing me his underwear, Lily.

LILY: It's Cuban?

SAM: Yeah, Cuban, Lily. One star, see? Five stripes. I special ordered it.

BOB: You can pull up your pants, Sam.

SAM: Right.

BOB: How was your walk, Lily?

LILY: It was good. I think I'll go back downstairs now.

BOB: Sure, that's a good idea. Why don't we all go downstairs? Get some coffee, huh, Sam? Get Molly up out of bed.

SAM: Yeah, just let me get these pants.

BOB: I'll get some shoes.

LILY: No, I'm not good company, Bob.

BOB: Huh?

LILY: You stay. You and Sam should talk.

BOB: I think we talked.

LILY: Sam, I'm very happy you and Bob are having this chance to reacquaint yourselves.

SAM: Well, sure.

LILY: No, I am. I think we're all going to have a happy weekend together. And by the end of the weekend there'll be no more awkwardness, nothing like that. We'll all be rested.

SAM: Uh huh.

LILY: *(To* BOB*)* I think I'll call David and Mary. I want to go downstairs and talk to David and Mary. Place a call.

BOB: Fine.

LILY: *(To* SAM*)* I woke up this morning missing the children. Their little voices. I'll be better company after I talk to the children.

SAM: I understand.

LILY: I'll see you boys downstairs.

SAM: Great. We'll see you downstairs.

LILY: Okay, Bob?

BOB: Fine, Lily.

LILY: I like your underwear, Sam.

SAM: Thanks, Lily.

(*Exit* LILY.)

(*Pause*)

SAM: Something seems wrong with Lily.

BOB: What seems?

SAM: It does. Seems wrong.

BOB: I think she just misses the children.

SAM: Uh huh.

(*Pause*)

(BOB *finds a pair of shoes. He puts them on.*)

SAM: In our business, Bob, a sad wife can be a dangerous thing.

BOB: Huh?

SAM: There are two things we don't like to talk about. Three things, Bob. Heart attacks, cancer and a wife who's decided somewhere down the road she can't be happy anymore.

BOB: She didn't decide.

SAM: I know that.

BOB: What did Lily decide?

SAM: No, things happen, Bob. Lots of things happen. They can leap out of nowhere. We don't even want to admit them, talk about them, nothing, because they can take you out of the picture. And the picture is business. We're meant to do business. It's fun. Every time I take a plane I look out the porthole and there's business. The fields, the desert, they're divided for business. Nothing is any longer just trees and bugs and animals. And there has to be a reason for that. Which is we need to take our minds off the things we can do absolutely

nothing about. Like if a car hits into us, or one of our
children. Or if the universe expands. Or detracts. Of
if a wife goes sad on us. Business is what protects us.
Because business is the only thing we have left to keep
our attention going and focused on something we can
do something about.

(Pause)

SAM: Lily's taking you out of the picture, Bob. From the
very beginning she took you out. There was no reason
you had to go to state college. You could have gone
away. You could have gone to the world.

(Pause)

SAM: Bob, on the way here yesterday we got lost. Molly
and I, in the car. And we argued. Our memories clashed
on which way we drove fifteen years ago. And finally
I pulled into this farmhouse. Nice white farmhouse
where there was no more farming. Just two guys living.
Young big fellows. Big plaid shirts. Healthy. No wives.
And they came out to ask what we wanted. These two
guys. So they gave us directions and we drove ahead.
But, Bob, it reminded me a hell of a lot, in the deepest
way, of what we used to have. When there were
directions, simple directions, anywhere you wanted to
go, and there were still all these choices. Simple choices.
Sometimes I think the promise I had, the expectation,
got interrupted when I married Molly.

(Pause)

SAM: I think you should tell me what's going on with
your wife.

(Pause)

BOB: Lily's been seeing buffalo, Sam.

SAM: What do you mean?

BOB: Buffalo.

SAM: What buffalo?

BOB: Buffalo, Sam. The animals that used to roam across America.

SAM: Oh.

BOB: She says they got loose. They're on the roads. They walk through buildings, cars. Like there's some kind of wide open prairie underneath our town. They walk through anything. Like it was never built. They can graze. They can graze anywhere they please. Once or twice they've been to our house.

SAM: The buffalo?

BOB: That's right.

SAM: You mean she's hallucinating.

BOB: Yes. She's hallucinating.

SAM: Jesus.

BOB: She's very concerned.

SAM: I can imagine.

BOB: She tried to hide it. It's been going on a year. She told me.

SAM: Yeah?

BOB: A whole year. She told me yesterday.

(*Pause*)

SAM: So what are you going to do about it?

BOB: I don't know.

SAM: Send her somewhere?

BOB: I don't know.

SAM: How about you? Do you see buffalo, Bob?

BOB: Me?

SAM: Yeah.

BOB: No. Of course I don't.

SAM: Okay.

BOB: Come on.

SAM: How about Indians?

BOB: What?

SAM: Does Lily sees Indians too?

BOB: No. Lily doesn't see Indians.

SAM: Uh huh.

BOB: What do you mean, does Lily see Indians?

SAM: Well, she reads, Bob. Lily reads a lot. Lily was always thinking about things more than we did. She was soft on animals, for example. Used to stand up for some of the losers. And that was great about Lily. How sensitive she was. But if she's taking it too far, well, then...

BOB: Sam, what are you talking about? Lily does not see Indians.

SAM: Well.

BOB: You think this is funny?

SAM: No, I'm trying to get into the spirit of the thing.

BOB: You're trying to be funny.

SAM: Bob, it's farfetched.

BOB: No. It makes sense.

SAM: What makes sense about seeing a buffalo?

BOB: She's my wife, Sam.

SAM: It's a fantasy land.

BOB: So?

SAM: It's farfetched. And my rule when you're confronted with something farfetched you have to get that first laugh in fast. You have to laugh at it. Or else it gets real. I mean, look what happened to Hitler. The Arabs, too. They let those lunatic Arabs get real.

BOB: Sam.

SAM: We need more humor. Western humor.

BOB: Sam, Lily's passive to this. Lily's the victim.

SAM: I know.

BOB: She's not out there looking to disrupt anything.

SAM: She's going to terrorize you anyway, Bob. She is. Unless you snap her out of it.

BOB: Fine.

SAM: No, Bob, if I were you, I'd take her to one side and say, Honey, see the Indian? And she'll say, What Indian? And crack a smile, Bob, smile for her. She's your lady. Tell her you see an Indian. Or an elephant. Try an elephant. Tell her the elephants are chasing the buffalo. Hell, Bob, there are all kinds of things out there. Hallucinations, certain mental perspectives, Islam, all kinds of things, complexity, milling around in the air out there. Stuff way beyond the pale of business and common sense. So make it simple. Make it fun. Snap her out of it, Bob. Cause Lily used to be so alive. Likea spark, I remember. Some kind of spark in the sky. A wish, I think. Cause I used to look up to Lily. I used to think there was a feeling to Lily. Some kind of fairy tale feeling. Yeah. Like it could all be true. That's what I used to feel. It could be true with Lily.

(Pause)

SAM: Our problem, Bob, is we were born on the same square.

BOB: The same square?

SAM: Uh huh. The exact same one.

BOB: I don't know what square you're talking about.

SAM: Sure, you do.

BOB: What square?

SAM: For instance we both wanted Lily.

BOB: You wanted Lily?

SAM: Yeah. Yeah, I think I can safely say I wanted Lily.
It's enough time later to say that.

BOB: I didn't realize you wanted Lily.

SAM: Did you realize you wanted my job?

BOB: Yeah. Yeah, I realized.

SAM: I thought so.

BOB: I wanted to go to Italy.

SAM: Right. And I wanted Lily.

(Pause)

BOB: Well. I don't think we should switch, Sam.

SAM: I don't either.

BOB: I like being with my wife.

SAM: I can imagine.

BOB: She's my world.

SAM: Sure. Lily could make you feel that way.

BOB: Uh huh.

SAM: I can imagine. Cause she was something.

BOB: She is something.

(Pause)

*(SAM goes to the balcony door. He opens it. He looks at the
door.)*

SAM: Bob, listen. I remember when we painted your
parents' house. We were up on ladders painting their
house. And Lily was down below. She was watching.
Keeping us company. And I think it was about the first
time you and she were together. I could tell you were
together. And I know it was funny. It was funny to joke
later about how I fell off the ladder. Cause we took it
like a couple of guys. Cracked Humpty Dumpty jokes.
Took a picture even. Reenacted it, the next day. But
actually I think my thoughts were pretty complicated
up there. Serious. And I had a concussion. I don't think
we realized, a concussion maybe, lying there on the
ground. And it's like that thing when you think you
might die. Or you're caught between two worlds.
Cause I don't remember the ground, or the lawn, any
of that. I remember, clearly, that I stood in the middle of
a field. I was standing distinctly in a field. In the middle
of nowhere. And I had in my hand a doorknob. That's
all I had. For some reason. No door, no house, just
the doorknob. And I could hear there was knocking.
Something was knocking. And then Lily came up to
me. In this field. And she said she noticed something.
She wanted to tell me. So I asked her what she noticed.
And she said, Out there, Sam, is a last good moment.
And I said, What? And she said, Out there, at the end
of the field. And she said it again, like I was dumb
or something. So I looked toward the end of the field,
to see if I could see this moment, whatever moment
she meant. And I saw there were trees and some pond
off to the side. And then I thought I noticed it too.
I thought I noticed what Lily noticed. And when
I realized that, the trees at the end of the field got
suddenly closer. I was standing right underneath them.
And then these things fell off me. Like my memory.
Like my understanding of why an airplane should
work or a car. Taxes. Doors. The doorknob. People
behaving on earth. Those kinds of understandings just

fell off me. Like a dirty T-shirt. Some kind of T-shirt.
And underneath was my chest. This feeling in my chest.
And I thought, Christ, I think I'm going to see
something. I'm going to see sights. I'm going to see
all kinds of shapes and sizes, things that hang out and
heave out there. Things behind what I think I see out
there. I'm going to see influences.

(Pause)

SAM: When I woke up on the ground at the foot of
your house, Bob, I saw Lily. She was leaning over me,
concerned. And behind her head was the sky. She was
with me beneath the sky. And I remember her eyes.
Like high school. Eager like high school. Like it was the
end, the end of all conception, or thinking, and at the
end was this eagerness. Waiting for me. This simplicity.

(Pause)

SAM: I think that hurt me. That simplicity.

(Pause)

SAM: I think sometimes about the inquisitor. The grand
inquisitor. What we read in school. That Russian book.
The guy who had to tell Christ that simplicity could
hurt people.

(Pause)

(SAM *closes the balcony door.)*

SAM: Personally, Bob. I'll tell you what I notice. What I
feel. I see a Doberman. I keep seeing this Doberman
follow me.

(Blackout)

END OF ACT ONE

ACT TWO

(Early evening)

*(*LILY *is in a slip. She is sitting at the dressing table, combing her hair.)*

(Pause)

(Enter BOB *through the open balcony door. He is dressed for dinner. He looks at* LILY.*)*

BOB: Honey?

LILY: Yes, Bob?

BOB: Honey, I think they're waiting.

LILY: I know.

BOB: Molly and Sam are probably waiting.

LILY: I'm almost done.

BOB: You don't even have your dress on.

LILY: It's on the bed.

BOB: What?

LILY: My dress is on the bed.

(Pause)

BOB: Lily, your hair is fine. You should leave your hair.

LILY: Bob.

BOB: I mean it. Your hair's great. It's always great.

LILY: I want to fix my hair.

(BOB *stands at the balcony door.*)

LILY: How is it outside?

BOB: Huh?

LILY: What's it like outside?

BOB: It's fine outside. *(He closes the balcony door. He comes into the room. He stands on the rug. He waits.)*

LILY: Mary's reading about the Argonauts. Remember the Argonauts, Bob?

BOB: The what?

LILY: The Greek Argonauts.

BOB: No, I don't.

LILY: Mary's homework this weekend concerns the Argonauts.

BOB: Oh.

LILY: She told me on the phone. She's reading where they're sailing past the Sirens. And Orpheus is singing.

BOB: Uh huh.

LILY: He's singing so his crew won't hear the Sirens.

BOB: I don't know these people, Lily.

LILY: You don't know the Sirens?

BOB: No.

LILY: You don't remember the ladies who lived on the rocks?

BOB: What rocks?

LILY: The island of rocks. The ones who lured sailors to their destruction.

BOB: I don't remember them.

LILY: Bob, it was in school.

BOB: School was a long time ago, Lily. Would you please finish your hair?

LILY: Well, that's what Mary and I talked about.

BOB: The Greeks from school?

LILY: Yes.

(Pause)

(BOB waits. He looks at the mirror. It's tilted. He goes to the bed. He unplugs the clock radio from the wall. He goes to the dressing table with the clock radio. He straightens the mirror. He leans the clock radio against it.)

BOB: Do you think you could go faster now?

LILY: I could have straightened the mirror, Bob.

BOB: You can see, Lily. That might be faster.

LILY: I wasn't ready to see.

BOB: No?

LILY: I wasn't, no.

BOB: Lily, I want you to go faster. I thought this would be faster.

(BOB stands behind LILY.)

(Pause)

BOB: I should have got you a brush. I'm sorry. A comb in your hair is ridiculous. It's like using a teaspoon. A teaspoon to shovel snow.

(The phone rings. BOB picks it up.)

BOB: *(Into phone)* Hello?...Yeah, hi...I know...I know, Sam...Right.

(BOB hangs up.)

BOB: Molly's ready.

LILY: Uh huh.

BOB: She's downstairs ready. She's starting to drink.

LILY: Uh huh, good.

BOB: Sam's running out of magazines.

LILY: Bob, what are you doing?

BOB: Huh?

LILY: You're acting something.

BOB: Just do your hair.

LILY: What kind of gesture is that?

BOB: Teaspoon.

LILY: What?

BOB: It's a teaspoon. I'm shoveling show with a teaspoon. Now would you mind?

(BOB *goes to the bathroom. He looks inside. He turns off the bathroom light. He steps into the room again. He sees* LILY's *pocketbook. He puts it on the bed with* LILY's *dress.*)

LILY: Bob, why don't you go downstairs and wait with them? I can get ready.

BOB: You can get ready?

LILY: You should wait with them.

BOB: No, I think I'll wait here.

LILY: You think that would be better?

BOB: Yes, I do. (*He looks at the Indian on the wall.*) This Indian reminds me of me. He does. His arms out, full moon, crying to the moon. (*He puts his arms out. He makes a face.*)

LILY: Have dinner without me, Bob.

BOB: Huh?

LILY: Don't you think you could have dinner without me? Tell them I have a headache. You've been up here trying to get rid of my headache.

BOB: But you don't have a headache.

LILY: I think I do, Bob.

BOB: Must be the comb.

LILY: The comb?

BOB: Pulling at your hair with the comb. That could be the headache.

LILY: I'm only going to get tired again.

BOB: At dinner?

LILY: I can feel it already. I'm very tired.

(Pause)

BOB: There's something intensely hostile about you at this moment.

LILY: I'm not hostile.

BOB: Oh, yes, you are.

LILY: I never wanted to come here in the first place.

BOB: That's hostile.

LILY: I don't think so.

BOB: Not wanting to return to the location of our honeymoon, to a reunion of our friends, that's not hostile?

LILY: It's not hostile.

BOB: Lily, finish your hair.

LILY: I don't want to finish my hair.

BOB: Then put your dress on.

LILY: I don't want to put my dress on.

BOB: Why not?

LILY: Because I'm still doing my hair.

(Pause)

BOB: There are times when I look at you and I swear you've been invaded. That some obnoxious spirit has taken command of your mind. And taken your whole body and dumped it underwater. Because you start to move slow. Everything gets slow. Resistant. Like you don't have the guts to tell me what's on your mind. You just get slow. Get tired. You take naps. Like this afternoon, Lily, that nap was ridiculous. It was ridiculous to disappear like that and take that nap.

(LILY picks up a towel. She takes either end of the towel in her hands and thoroughly messes up and tangles her hair with the towel. She puts the towel down. She picks up the comb again and slowly starts to untangle her hair.)

(Pause)

(BOB is astonished.)

BOB: I have never in my life seen you ever do anything like that.

LILY: I'm being nice about it, Bob.

BOB: Nice?

LILY: I could have been nasty all afternoon. Instead I was nice.

BOB: You weren't nice. You took a nap.

LILY: That was nice.

BOB: It wasn't nice, Lily. That was rude.

LILY: No, Bob. I could have been rude.

BOB: Could have been?

LILY: Much ruder, yes. You've never seen what I could have been this afternoon.

(*Pause*)

BOB: I think I will go downstairs and have dinner with my friends.

LILY: Really?

BOB: I think so.

LILY: Fine. Have dinner.

BOB: Do you think you might be finished by the time I have dinner? Finished with your hair? This mood?

LILY: This isn't a mood.

BOB: No?

LILY: I'm angry.

BOB: Well, that's a mood.

LILY: No, I'm specifically angry.

BOB: Specifically?

LILY: You like specifics.

BOB: I know.

LILY: I thought so.

BOB: Well, that's good, Lily. It's good you're specific.

LILY: Yes.

BOB: I'm glad. Because maybe by the time I return from dinner, maybe by then you could just kill me off, instead of playing with me like a cat. In the meantime, however, I intend to have dinner with my friends.

(BOB *pulls open the door to the hallway. He exits. He slams the door behind him.* LILY *jumps up. She goes to the door. She pulls it open.*)

LILY: *(Shouting down the hall)* YOUR STUPID, JERK, SLIMY FRIEND ASKED IF I COULD SEE ANY INDIANS!

(LILY slams the door. She locks it. She takes MOLLY's damp chair and places it against the door. The door knob turns. It's locked.)

(Pause)

BOB: *(From off)* Lily, open the door.

LILY: No.

BOB: *(From off)* Let me in.

LILY: No.

BOB: *(From off)* I want to talk.

LILY: Go to dinner.

BOB: *(From off)* I don't want dinner.

LILY: Go to dinner with your friends.

BOB: *(From off)* Lily, come on, people can hear out here.

LILY: I don't want to go to dinner!

BOB: *(From off)* You don't have to go to dinner!

(Pause)

BOB: *(From off)* Lily, come on. Let me in. Please. We don't have to go to dinner. We can stay in the room. We can be quiet. Lily, you can do your hair. You can do your hair forever. Just let me in the room. I like your hair. I love your hair. I love your hair very much.

(Pause)

(LILY unlocks the door. She goes away from the door. BOB pushes the door against MOLLY's chair. He enters the room. He closes the door.)

BOB: Sam asked if you could see any Indians?

LILY: Yes.

BOB: Any particular Indians?

LILY: You know what kind of Indians.

BOB: No, I don't.

LILY: Bob, I can't go to dinner with somebody who's going to be looking at me all the time waiting for me to see a buffalo.

BOB: Lily.

LILY: You had no business telling Sam.

BOB: He's my friend.

LILY: He's not my friend.

BOB: He asked, dammit.

LILY: He did? Did he ask does your wife have visions of buffalo?

BOB: No, I was upset.

LILY: How dare you give Sam the opportunity?

BOB: Please. He's trying to be funny.

LILY: Sam doesn't know how to be funny.

BOB: No, I know.

LILY: You're lucky, Bob, I took a nap.

BOB: Okay.

LILY: Compared to what could have happened, we're lucky.

BOB: I know. I'm sorry.

(Pause)

(LILY goes to the dressing table. She sits down. She combs her hair.)

LILY: I think you get invaded by a spirit yourself. The whole weekend you've been invaded. Otherwise why would you tell Sam about what I see? And why would you tell me about Laurie? How he uses Laurie. How do you expect me to sit still at the same table with this man? How do you expect me to do anything except be upset with this man? I think, Bob, if we were really to get specific about this weekend, really specific about the moods going on, then I think we'd have to say you want Sam or me to decide something for you. You can't seem to decide something anymore.

(Pause)

(BOB *takes* MOLLY's *damp chair and pushes it to the bed. He sits down next to the bed.*)

BOB: This is where I sat this afternoon, when I found you here in bed. I almost woke you, I was so angry. But instead I took this chair, Molly's chair, and sat in it. I watched you sleep. And then I got tired. Real tired myself. So I got up and got into bed with you. And fell asleep. I had a dream I couldn't get into our house. My own home. Everything was locked, the door, the windows. So I started screaming and shouting. I thought David or Mary could let me in. Instead what happened is I saw you upstairs. In our bedroom. You were brushing your hair. And the more I hollered the more you brushed your hair. Until finally I ran out of hollering and you got up and came to the window upstairs. I think you came to the window to tell me how to get in. But by the time you got to the window, you were bald. Your head was totally bald. *(Pause)* When I woke up the first word that occurred to me was "Rapunzel".

LILY: Uh huh.

BOB: Which probably means I'm in some kind of trouble.

LILY: Why?

BOB: Well, a bald Rapunzel.

LILY: I think you couldn't rescue me. In your dream.

BOB: I couldn't rescue you?

LILY: I don't think so.

BOB: I wasn't trying to rescue you, Lily. I was trying
to get into the house. My own house. *(Pause)* Lily,
I happen to be extremely frightened right now.
I am frightened. *(Pause)* I feel like we had a boat.
Once upon a time a boat. We sheltered each other in
this boat. We built it, we took care. And all the rest of
life, Engelbetter, governments, all those bigger things
didn't matter, because you and I, we were crossing the
ocean together. I was so proud to cross this ocean. But
what seems to be happening to you, Lily, and how I can
do nothing to help, that's making me feel very small.
And when you talk about hallucinating, and being
tired, and not wanting to go to dinner, I feel like a tiny,
tiny person. A dot. A tiny dot that bops up and down.
Because the boat is gone. The usual things we used
to do are gone. And all I have are thoughts. My tiny
thoughts to protect me. To keep me bopping up and
down. Because underneath is the ocean. The big ocean.
And huge currents. Big mindless things that move
me around. Cause I left land with you, Lily. I left land.
I thought there was another land.

(Pause)

(LILY goes to BOB.)

LILY: I think we should go to dinner.

BOB: You do?

LILY: Yes, I do.

BOB: Lily, I'm sorry about Sam.

LILY: I know.

BOB: I need your love again, Lily, I do. Your attention.

LILY: I know, I do.

(BOB & LILY *embrace.*)

(*There is a knock on the door.*)

(*Pause*)

LILY: It's them.

BOB: I'll see who it is.

(BOB *goes to the door. He opens it.* SAM & MOLLY *stand in the hall.*)

BOB: Sam?

SAM: (*From off*) Bob?

BOB: Hi, Sam.

SAM: (*From off*) Bob, we're ready.

BOB: Great.

SAM: (*From off*) Are you ready?

BOB: No. No, we're not ready.

SAM: (*From off*) Well, come on.

LILY: (*Taking her dress*) Bob, I'm going into the bathroom.

BOB: What, Lily?

LILY: (*Exiting*) The bathroom.

BOB: Sure. (*To* SAM) Lily's in the bathroom.

SAM: (*From off*) Yeah?

BOB: She's almost ready.

SAM: (*From off*) Is Lily okay?

BOB: Sure. Sure, Lily's okay.

SAM: (*From off*) Come on. You can tell.

BOB: Sam, Lily's fine.

MOLLY: *(From off)* What's the matter with Lily?

BOB: Nothing, Molly. Lily's getting ready in the bathroom. That's all. We'll all be ready very soon.

MOLLY: *(From off)* Can we come in?

BOB: Huh?

MOLLY: *(From off)* Can we come in and wait?

BOB: You want to do that?

SAM: *(From off)* Molly wants to come in, Bob.

MOLLY: *(From off)* I don't like it out here.

SAM: *(From off)* She doesn't like the hall.

BOB: Well, what about downstairs? You were waiting downstairs?

SAM: *(From off)* Molly doesn't like it downstairs.

BOB: No?

MOLLY: *(From off)* Bob, please.

BOB: Yeah, well, Lily's in the bathroom.

MOLLY: *(From off)* Please. We've been waiting so long.

BOB: Well, sure. Come on in. Just let me tell Lily.

(SAM & MOLLY walk in. MOLLY holds a drink.)

(BOB goes to the bathroom. He knocks on the door.)

BOB: Lily? Lily, everybody's here.

SAM: That's right, Lily, we're here.

BOB: Sam and Molly are here.

SAM: We're waiting.

BOB: Lily?

SAM: As a matter of fact, Lily, we're lighting a fire. We're lighting a goddam fire under your fanny.

(BOB *steps away from the bathroom.*)

BOB: Well, this is good. That's good, she'll be ready soon. See, Lily forgot her hairbrush, that's one problem. It's been a problem. It's been a problem all weekend.

MOLLY: That's okay, Bob. We've had several problems this weekend, Sam and I. For example, I had a dream this morning, a nasty dream, about that restaurant. I'm not even sure we should go there.

BOB: The restaurant downstairs?

MOLLY: Yes, that one.

BOB: You don't want to go there?

MOLLY: Well, it was nasty.

BOB: Really? I thought we had a good time. (*To* SAM) Didn't we have a good time?

MOLLY: Sam did, I think.

BOB: Is there another restaurant or something?

MOLLY: I don't know. Is there, Sam?

SAM: What's the matter with the restaurant, Molly?

MOLLY: Nothing, Sam.

SAM: It's late to switch restaurants.

BOB: I'm sorry to hear this.

MOLLY: It's all right, Bob. I'm sure Sam is right. It's late.

SAM: I'm not switching.

MOLLY: No, I'm sure we shouldn't. Let's not switch.

SAM: Good.

MOLLY: Sam knows how to do this, Bob. Sam knows how to get us downstairs. We should listen.

BOB: Yeah.

(Pause)

(MOLLY *picks up the clock radio. The mirror tilts.*
She puts the radio down.)

MOLLY: It was quite nasty, though, this dream. I must
say. Nasty. We were at the table downstairs and, Bob,
you were pouring wine and speaking German.

BOB: German, really?

MOLLY: Yes. I was quite impressed.

BOB: That's funny. Speaking German.

MOLLY: I know. But then Sam started speaking German
too. And then Lily. And for a while I got scared, I didn't
say anything, I thought I might be left speaking English
all by myself. But when I opened my mouth, sure
enough, I spoke German too.

BOB: German, huh? You mean we understood each
other?

MOLLY: Oh, yes. We did. It was wonderful. We were all
quite suddenly fluent in German.

BOB: Yeah.

MOLLY: The wine too. The wine got German. Mosel.
And Sam's car. I remember that was parked outside
and it turned German. It became a Porsche. With tractor
wheels. And we were all looking out the window,
commenting on Sam's new tractor wheels. In German,
of course, and Sam was telling us he was thinking of
installing a periscope. When all of a sudden Lily leaned
forward and informed us that the restaurant wasn't
safe. She did. In fact, she said the whole inn had become
dangerous. The building. Because there were other
Germans outside. Real Germans roaming around in
the countryside. And these Germans, they were Nazis,
Lily said, and I remember Lily suggested we get out of

there before they arrived. So we all ran out the
restaurant and out the front door. Except I didn't make
it. Because I saw a bathroom, which I needed to go to.
And then in the bathroom I heard this pounding. These
Germans pounding on the door. And that made me
scared. Until suddenly I realized, oh, no, wait a minute.
It's 1980. 1980. What are these people doing here? So I
flung open the bathroom door and I screamed at these
Nazis, I screamed it's 1980! You're all gone! So go away!
   But they didn't listen. These people, they captured me
instead.

BOB: Hm.

MOLLY: Then I woke up. I woke up feeling very
captured.

BOB: Yeah.

MOLLY: Well, don't be embarrassed, Bob. It's only a
dream.

BOB: I know. Of course.

MOLLY: I was captured, that's all. All day I've been
captured. Feeling captured. I was getting especially
captured downstairs. Waiting.

BOB: I'm sorry.

MOLLY: Then those people started to sneer.

BOB: What people?

MOLLY: At the desk. Sam ordered a drink. They sneered.

SAM: I thought they snickered.

MOLLY: They did that too.

SAM: Snickered and sneered, huh?

MOLLY: Yes, you should realize what goes on behind
your back.

SAM: *(To BOB)* Boy. Pretty busy downstairs.

MOLLY: *(To* BOB*)* I think these people get away with stuff because Sam is so frontwards.

SAM: Frontwards, Molly?

MOLLY: Yes, you're intent on what's in front of you.

SAM: Then what about my job?

BOB: *(At the bathroom door)* Lily?

SAM: My job, Molly? How do you suppose I do as well as I do at that? *(To* BOB*)* This is the sort of thing Molly can't answer.

MOLLY: Sam, your job is based on the concept of frontwards, didn't you tell me that? It has nothing to do with a real world.

SAM: *(To* BOB*)* Tonight is not going to be charming.

BOB: Ah, listen, are you sure you guys don't want to wait downstairs?

MOLLY: Again?

BOB: Or in your room, I don't know.

MOLLY: Bob, I don't like our room. I think it's got smaller.

BOB: Your room is smaller?

MOLLY: Than last time, yes.

SAM: Molly thinks they subdivided it.

MOLLY: I do not.

SAM: Then how did it get smaller?

MOLLY: I'm not talking about reality, Sam. I'm talking about an emotional terrain.

SAM: Emotional what?

MOLLY: Terrain. An impression. My memory. I remember bigger rooms. I remember much more space.

A sense of horizon. Distance. Furtherwhich, I don't remember this color either.

SAM: Furtherwhich, Molly?

MOLLY: This pale brown. I remember blue. There were big blue walls and big wide windows. A bigger balcony. This rug too, it was bigger. In fact, the whole building seems to have shrunk. Even the people downstairs, they seem irritated. Don't you find them irritated? Small?

BOB: I hadn't, no.

MOLLY: Bob, I remember people who were happy. Like us. Eager. People with smooth faces. And a big smile. And they used to have a bell, a shiny little bell on the counter, you could push it whenever you wanted their attention.

SAM: No, Molly. I saw the bell.

MOLLY: Well, then. It's my memory, isn't it?

SAM: I guess so.

MOLLY: My memory has been expectant. My memory contains something that has been taken away. Something maybe more serious, far more serious, than just a shiny little bell.

(Pause)

BOB: Ah, listen, maybe I should just go in and see what's holding up, Lily.

SAM: Yeah, you should go in.

BOB: Good.

MOLLY: We'll wait out here, Bob.

BOB: That's good.

MOLLY: Great, Bob.

BOB: Listen, if you need to go downstairs or anything, if you need to start up at the restaurant, that's fine, I understand.

SAM: Thanks, we're fine.

BOB: Okay, then.

SAM: Tell Lily from me the fire's getting hot.

BOB: What fire?

SAM: The fire under her fanny.

BOB: Right. I'll tell her.

SAM: Great.

(BOB *knocks on the bathroom door. He opens it. He exits into the bathroom.)*

(Pause)

MOLLY: Sam, I think you should encourage Bob to relax and have fun. Instead of rushing him.

SAM: This isn't fun.

MOLLY: No, it is. I think any time four people can't make it to dinner, that's fun.

SAM: Molly, I know what's fun.

MOLLY: Cuba, dear?

SAM: Cuba?

MOLLY: I don't think your underwear is such fun.

SAM: Molly, I'm sick of these insinuations. To talk about the size of the room the way you do, the shiny little bell downstairs, all of that, my underwear, that's insinuating.

MOLLY: What was I insinuating?

SAM: A certain disappointment.

MOLLY: No, Sam. I'm being quite clear.

SAM: Molly.

MOLLY: I'm in earnest, no. It's perfectly obvious to all of us we're disappointed.

SAM: Listen, why don't you just take a seat in your chair?

MOLLY: Excuse me?

SAM: Your chair. Have a chair while we wait for Lily.

MOLLY: I don't like that chair.

SAM: Sure, you do.

MOLLY: You poured water on that chair.

SAM: I did?

MOLLY: In front of us all. Your poured your glass.

SAM: It wasn't water.

MOLLY: Well, whatever. I never understood why you poured.

SAM: You said it was damp. You insisted. So I made it damp.

MOLLY: The chair?

SAM: That's right.

MOLLY: The chair was already damp. You made it wet.

SAM: No, Molly.

MOLLY: Yes. This chair was damp. Lily left it out in the drizzle.

SAM: The what?

MOLLY: The drizzle. That particular weekend it drizzled, I remember, on the balcony. Lily left it out in the drizzle.

SAM: It didn't drizzle.

MOLLY: It did something.

SAM: There wasn't even a dew, for christsakes.

MOLLY: There was something out there.

SAM: What, a tall dog? Did a tall dog jump up and drizzle?

MOLLY: Sam, to this day I still don't understand what decided you to pour your glass.

SAM: Well, Molly, if I remember, I decided reality and your perception of reality were out of sync. So I did the only thing I could to let them catch up with each other. I poured bourbon on the chair.

MOLLY: No wonder they snicker downstairs.

SAM: Maybe so, Molly. But, listen, I can tell you one thing for sure. I can tell you this chair isn't damp anymore.

MOLLY: That's nice.

SAM: So take a seat.

MOLLY: Stop trying to boss me.

SAM: I want you to take a seat.

MOLLY: What for?

SAM: *(Taking* MOLLY *by the arm)* Just take a seat.

MOLLY: Sam.

SAM: Take a seat.

(SAM finds a pressure point in MOLLY's arm.
He sits MOLLY down in the chair.)

(Pause)

SAM: Are we going to go through this again?

MOLLY: You hurt my arm.

SAM: Are we going to live through one of these scenes where you challenge me in front of a friend?

MOLLY: My arm, Sam. I am sick of living with a man who's so utterly frontwards.

SAM: Molly, don't use frontwards.

MOLLY: Why not? It's what I mean.

SAM: It sounds baby.

MOLLY: You don't want to hear.

SAM: If you want me to hear, then speak clearly to me as an adult.

MOLLY: Very well.

SAM: I am not your father. You can't appeal to me, or lull me, with baby terminology. Frontwards, for example. Furtherwhich.

MOLLY: I see.

SAM: You can't explain to me that rooms shrink.

MOLLY: Fine. Then let's call it peripheral vision.

SAM: That's better.

MOLLY: Your peripheral vision has atrophied.

SAM: Good.

MOLLY: You can only see what's in front of you. You cannot see what's to the side or behind or how any of that deeply influences what you perceive as being in front of you.

SAM: Fine. My peripheral vision has atrophied. We're doing very well in this world anyway.

MOLLY: Are we talking about your job again?

SAM: Yes, my job.

MOLLY: What's this obsession you have with your job?

SAM: I like to point it out to you.

MOLLY: Sometimes, really, you fail to realize that your job has about as much significance as a small sonata would to the Turkish people.

SAM: My job, huh?

MOLLY: You job, Sam, is based on the precept that peripheral vision is something that should be annihilated. That any notion of side effect, or backlash, is an idea to be crushed, or considered as emanating from another planet. Furthermore, Sam, ever since we went to Italy your self-importance and lack of humor have busted even their old bounds. You've developed the idea that there are certain people with dark faces who take pictures of you and follow your movements. You've even decided to talk your company into hiring security for you. All of which is not fun. In fact, history is filled with people like you. Filled with the rampages of certain humorless mini-minds who loved to be attended to by bodyguards.

(Pause)

SAM: Are you trying to be clever? Succinct?

MOLLY: You wanted me to talk like an adult.

SAM: Yes, I did.

MOLLY: Then make up your mind. Either you want me to talk like a child, you want me to submerge my intelligence. Or else you want me to talk like an adult. An intelligent human being who can ask for something logically and clearly and expect to receive it.

(Pause)

SAM: I'd give a lot more credence to what you say, all your clever little remarks, your put downs, if I didn't know that deep down you like to be pushed around.

MOLLY: That's not true.

SAM: It is true. That's what you want from a man. You want to be pushed around. Submerged. All this intelligence is a fantasy land. It's like your spots. It's a come on. You want somebody to take your snotty little nose and rub it in the world.

MOLLY: Sam.

SAM: Sit down.

MOLLY: Excuse me?

SAM: I said, Sit back down.

(SAM *pushes* MOLLY *back down into the chair.*)

(*Pause.* MOLLY *stands up again.*)

MOLLY: I don't see spots anymore, Sam. I don't let you chase them for me. I don't. Nor do I let you finish my sentences. My thoughts. I used to. I used to want your attention. Very much. And I think that's what happened to this chair. This chair was a puddle of water. I wanted you to lay down your coat for me. So I could cross over the water. So I could join your friends. Like Queen Elizabeth and Walter Raleigh. But you never dried the chair. You just made it wetter. And I think this chair now represents a swamp to me. A bog. A very deep bog which shifts. It festers. I think it's filled with stuff I no longer care enough to say to you. So don't you dare keep trying to shove me back down into it. (*Pause*) I think I'd like to go to the bathroom now.

SAM: The bathroom?

MOLLY: I must use the bathroom.

SAM: Sure.

MOLLY: I must be more kind to you, I think. You should be kind too.

SAM: Yeah?

MOLLY: We've both made a terrible mistake.

SAM: What mistake?

MOLLY: Let's be kind to each other, Sam. It'll help if we're kind.

SAM: Okay.

MOLLY: Good. We'll be kind. *(She exits.)*

(Pause)

(SAM stands in the middle of the room on the rug. BOB opens the bathroom door. He knocks. He comes in.)

BOB: Lily's on her way out.

SAM: Uh huh.

BOB: Real soon.

SAM: Good.

BOB: Where's Molly?

SAM: The bathroom.

BOB: Molly's in the bathroom?

SAM: Uh huh. They're both in the bathroom.

BOB: Boy.

SAM: Yeah. So when Lily gets out, we can go over to my bathroom and wait there.

BOB: Okay.

SAM: Don't worry. We'll get to dinner.

BOB: I know.

SAM: Rough night.

BOB: Yeah.

(They stand together on the rug.)

(Pause)

BOB: Do you ever feel, Sam, that underneath you is the ocean?

SAM: Huh?

BOB: The ocean, Sam.

SAM: What about the ocean?

BOB: That this is a little boat, this room, this life, even the planet, and underneath is the ocean. A huge ocean.

SAM: No, Bob.

BOB: Big fish. Planets. Sharks. Preordainment.

SAM: You imagine that beneath this rug?

BOB: Well, anywhere, Sam.

SAM: No, I don't.

BOB: Uh huh. What do you imagine?

SAM: I imagine a Latin American country.

BOB: Pardon?

SAM: Latin America, Bob. My life with Molly is Latin America. It's like putting down one revolution after another. Like spots. I suppress spots, but then snickers break out. People sneer. Then the rooms shrink. And shiny little bells disappear off of front desks. And on top of everything Molly's decided to mention a mistake.

BOB: What mistake?

SAM: I don't know. I have to ask her.

BOB: That's on your mind, huh?

SAM: Molly, yeah. This mistake.

BOB: You want to know what's on my mind?

SAM: Sure.

BOB: Okay. How come you asked my wife if she could see any Indians?

SAM: How come?

BOB: That's on my mind.

SAM: I was trying to be helpful, Bob.

BOB: I don't think it helped.

SAM: No, I know.

BOB: She's in the bathroom now.

SAM: Right.

BOB: What prompted you to help?

SAM: She didn't seem like she was paying attention.

BOB: Attention to what?

SAM: Bob, I'm sorry. Look, I'm sorry I said anything to Lily. I just had a flash, that's all, sitting there with Lily. A flash that I could say the right thing. That seemed so clear to me, it did, and this comment about Crazy Horse jumped out of my mouth. It just did.

BOB: Crazy Horse?

SAM: Yeah, I asked her to take me to Crazy Horse.

BOB: She didn't tell me about that.

SAM: Well, I was trying to be funny, Bob.

BOB: Why Crazy Horse?

SAM: What do you mean, why?

BOB:Why not Pocahontas?

SAM: Pocahontas didn't come to mind.

BOB: Crazy Horse did?

SAM: Bob, what is this? I just said I'm sorry.

BOB: I'm not sure, Sam. I'm not sure what it is you're sorry about.

SAM: I'm sorry about what I said.

BOB: No, I think you meant it. Deep down you meant it.

SAM: Yeah? What deep down did I mean?

BOB: I don't know. You tell me, buddy.

(Enter LILY *from the bathroom.)*

(Pause)

LILY: I'm ready for dinner, Bob.

BOB: She's ready, Sam.

LILY: Hello, Sam.

SAM: Great. I'll get Molly.

LILY: That's a nice jacket, Sam.

SAM: Yeah?

LILY: Dinner jacket, yes. Yellow jacket.

SAM: Thank you.

BOB: Yeah, Sam, did anyone ever tell you, you kind of remind a person of General Custer?

SAM: Excuse me?

BOB: Yeah, if you had curly yellow locks and tighter pants, you'd look exactly like General Custer. George Custer comes to mind.

SAM: Really, Bob?

BOB: I mean, if you were thinner and taller and your hair were yellow.

SAM: That's a long way to go, Bob.

BOB: No, I think you have the same kind of spirit.

SAM: As Custer, huh?

BOB: Yeah, the same spirit.

LILY: Bob, I thought we were going to dinner. You wanted dinner.

SAM: What spirit are you talking about, Bob?

BOB: I don't know, Sam, the rape spirit, I think. Rape the land, bomb the Cubans, that kind of spirit.

SAM: Uh huh.

BOB: The kind of spirit that could ask your secretary to screw up the basic trust that people have to have to do business with each other. Cause it's people like you, your kind of hotshot that gets to the top, that's what screws the rest of us up. Cause you come on through, you make a few quick killings, and by the time people catch on, you're gone. You're like sharks. You have to keep moving or you can't breathe. You're dead. Meanwhile the rest of us have to clean up after you. The rest of us have to regain the trust below, the trust you violated to get to the top.

LILY: Maybe I should get Molly. Go wait with Molly.

BOB: Lily, that's fine. (To SAM) And what really pisses me off is you get a bodyguard. Sam Kass gets a bodyguard.

SAM: It's the way things are.

BOB: Bodyguard. Like it's some kind of new title.

SAM: We're an American company, Bob. It's a foreign world.

BOB: Sam, you're sounding very stupid.

SAM: The world is stupid.

BOB: I'm not stupid.

SAM: Me neither.

BOB: You are stupid. Your behavior is stupid.

SAM: Bob, I don't think my behavior is half as stupid as what you're doing here with Lily.

BOB: Oh, yeah?

SAM: This behavior is stupid. It's stupid to dig a hole and climb into it. It's stupid to hole up in here and talk about the angry voices outside. The invisible enemy. The Indians lined up in the sky. The little mental arrows. Cause you used to have assurance. You used to know who the enemy was. The most assurance of anybody I knew. But I think something's gone in you. Whipped, or winded, I don't know. Cause you're nothing like the last time we were together in this room. And as for your wife, Bob. Bob, tell her we killed the buffalo. Tell Lily they're dead. There's no point in seeing them anymore.

BOB: Get out of my room, Sam.

SAM: The two of you are wimps. Utter wimps compared to what you used to be.

BOB: Get out.

SAM: What for?

BOB: I don't want you in this room.

LILY: Bob.

BOB: Get out, Sam.

SAM: Bob, you're a wimp. Don't try to tell me to get out.

(BOB *starts for* SAM.)

LILY: *(Intervening)* Bob.

BOB: Lily, come on.

LILY: Bob, this is silly. Isn't it silly?

BOB: Sam, get out of my room.

LILY: Sam, please.

SAM: How can I get out of this room? How can I be bossed out of this room?

BOB: Cause it's my room.

LILY: Bob.

SAM: It's his room, Lily. He's going to have to get me out.

BOB: You bet, Sam.

LILY: *(Pounding on* BOB*)* Dammit, Bob! Dammit! You stop it.

*(*LILY *kicks* BOB *in the shins. He looks at her in amazement.* LILY *picks up a chair and faces* SAM*.)*

LILY: You too, Sam. You stop trying to slug each other.

BOB: Lily, put the chair down.

LILY: No.

BOB: Put it down. You're just adding to the tension in this room.

LILY: No, I'm not. I'm going to smash the tension.

BOB: You're going to smash it, huh?

LILY: Right on the head.

BOB: Uh huh.

SAM: Leave her, Bob.

BOB: What?

SAM: Don't try to disarm your wife.

BOB: Sam, you called me a wimp.

SAM: I know. I meant it too.

BOB: Right.

SAM: So you want to go outside?

BOB: Outside?

SAM: You want to go politely around Lily? Go outside?

BOB: Yeah. Yeah, I'd like to go outside.

SAM: Good. Let's go outside. Let's go on the lawn.

BOB: Right. The lawn.

(BOB *walks in a circle around* LILY.)

(SAM *opens the hallway door. He exits.*)

BOB: I'll be right back, Lily.

LILY: Are we going to dinner?

BOB: I don't know. Depends who's the wimp.

LILY: You don't have to hit him, Bob.

BOB: Lily, somebody's got to hit this guy before he gets a bodyguard.

LILY: Bob.

(BOB *embraces* LILY. *He kisses her.*)

BOB: Bye, Lily. *(He exits.)*

(Pause)

(LILY *looks at the empty room. Enter* MOLLY.)

MOLLY: You know the oddest thing happened.

LILY: What happened?

MOLLY: I was in the bathroom just now, my bathroom, and I thought I heard somebody knocking.

LILY: On the bathroom?

MOLLY: Yes, knocking. A distinct knocking. But I opened the door and no one was there.

LILY: No one rushed out, you think?

MOLLY: Where's my husband?

LILY: He's outside. Both of them.

MOLLY: I see. What about dinner?

LILY: I don't know.

MOLLY: What's happening outside?

LILY: I think they're going to square off.

MOLLY: Really?

(LILY & MOLLY *go to the balcony door. They look out.*)

(*Pause*)

MOLLY: They don't seem to be doing much.

LILY: They're talking.

MOLLY: That's good.

LILY: We'll let them talk.

MOLLY: Yes. They don't seem so big anymore.

LILY: Our husbands?

MOLLY: Yes, at least from here.

LILY: You thought they were big?

MOLLY: Well, this weekend. That was big.

LILY: Yes, it was. Very big.

(*They look out the balcony door.*)

(*Pause*)

MOLLY: I think you have a wonderful husband.

LILY: Thank you.

MOLLY: No, I do. Your husband is very attentive.

(*Pause*)

LILY: Maybe after they talk, maybe I'll feel easier.
I'll feel easier around Sam.

MOLLY: Maybe.

LILY: Because I like you, Molly. I like you so much
more than I imagined.

MOLLY: Good.

LILY: I like how you talk.

MOLLY: You do?

LILY: Oh, yes. You're articulate.

MOLLY: I don't think I'm articulate.

LILY: No, I like how you stand up to Sam.

MOLLY: I don't stand up.

LILY: I think you did.

(Pause)

(They step away from the balcony.)

LILY: Is Sam really going to hire a plainclothes man?

MOLLY: That's right.

LILY: When you get back to Italy, you will be followed by a plainclothes man?

MOLLY: Sam will be followed.

LILY: Is he really in danger?

MOLLY: He might be.

LILY: Somebody might kidnap him? Or kill him someday?

MOLLY: Yes.

LILY: Some angry foreigner?

MOLLY: Probably.

LILY: Why would they want to do that?

MOLLY: He represents us.

LILY: Sam represents us?

MOLLY: That's right. He does.

(Pause)

LILY: What's it like to live with a man who represents us?

MOLLY: It scares me.

LILY: Yes.

MOLLY: It's starting to scare me.

(Pause)

(LILY *drifts back toward the balcony.*)

MOLLY: Does this room seem smaller to you?

LILY: I don't know. Maybe.

MOLLY: I think so too.

LILY: Molly?

MOLLY: What?

LILY: Do you see that cloud over there?

MOLLY: Uh huh.

LILY: Over the tree?

MOLLY: Yes.

LILY: What does that look like to you?

MOLLY: I don't know. Buffalo?

(Pause)

(Lights go down.)

(Blackout)

END OF PLAY

PLAYWRIGHT'S NOTE

Five years ago was when I first started work on THE
LAST GOOD MOMENT OF LILY BAKER. Actually,
I was working on another play. Something called
TIMOTHY'S NUCLEAR STRATEGY. But in the middle
of struggling with TIMOTHY, I found myself writing
down stretches of dialogue and monologue that
belonged to something quite clearly separate. There
was the name Lily. The names Bob and Sam. And I
liked how they talked to each other. They talked in a
way that, on the surface, seemed flat. Almost corporate.
But I found it eloquent. Almost lyrical. Because their
manner of speech could not seem to acknowledge that
there might be trouble up ahead. Something wrong
between them. Because everything is supposed to be
fine. It is fine.

I think most of us have certain landmarks in our lives,
guidelines, things we live by, which we consider or
believe to be true. And then there are times, sometimes
whole years in our lives, when the landmarks suddenly
fail. The landmark may still be there, but now it seems
to lead up this strange street. This unfamiliar place,
where the old guidelines and expectations don't seem
to work anymore. And then there is a bitterness. Fear.
How did the landmark fail? Did it shift somehow?
Did the whole landscape change and we didn't notice?

I think as a nation too, we have experienced this.

I went to school and grew up mainly in Europe and the Middle East. I was aware, as a boy, of the mixed feelings other nations held toward my country, which at the time, the 50s and 60s, was still very much the dominant influence in the world. But I had no idea that beneath the mainly calm surface of information we receive everyday, no idea there could be such an accumulated anger toward us. This anger became utterly clear when on November 4, 1979, the United States Embassy in Teheran was taken over by Iranian militants.

I suspect the world, these days, is moving on a bit from blaming everything on the Western Powers, or those who benefited once upon a time from a simpler, more colonial world, in particular the United States. And certainly LILY BAKER makes no mention of the U S embassy in Teheran, even though the play takes place seven months later.

But then there is no mention of many things in this play. Because they are implicit. And in the end what's implicit, what's been there all along, can begin to surface. It can seep into a once familiar room and change it. Change the very ground we walk on. Shift landmarks while we didn't notice.

At the end of LILY BAKER some of the characters do begin to notice. They notice a shift. They begin to find words for it.

I would just like to add, finally, that I believe strongly in affirmation. I believe utterly there is a happy end. But I think sometimes happy ends must be found outside some of the structures, some of the roles we have chosen for ourselves. Because some of these choices can turn out to have been an imposition. A diminution of what our inner spirit may have originally wanted. And what I think is happy, what I find affirmative, is that no matter what the falling

structure may be, no matter what the role we must
cease to identify with, our ability to love, and to care
for each other, can be found be very much alive.
Completely intact.

Russell Davis
St Louis, 1989